A BALANCED MATHEMATICS PROGRAM INTEGRATING SCIENCE AND LANGUAGE ARTS

Unit Resource Guide
Unit 1

Populations and Samples

THIRD EDITION

KENDALL/HUNT PUBLISHING COMPANY
4050 Westmark Drive   Dubuque, Iowa 52002

A TIMS® Curriculum
University of Illinois at Chicago

UIC The University of Illinois
at Chicago

The original edition was based on work supported by the National Science Foundation under grant
No. MDR 9050226 and the University of Illinois at Chicago. Any opinions, findings, and conclusions
or recommendations expressed in this publication are those of the author(s) and do not necessarily
reflect the views of the granting agencies.

Printed in the United States of America

1 2 3 4 5 6 7 8 9 10   11 10 09 08 07

Letter Home

Populations and Samples

Date: _____

Dear Family Member:

Welcome to *Math Trailblazers®: A Balanced Mathematics Program Integrating Science and Language Arts.* Over the course of the year we will use math to solve many different kinds of problems. As we do this, your child will develop necessary math skills and experience how math is used to solve real-world problems.

This unit begins with a brief study of the number of eyelets in students' shoes. This investigation introduces the TIMS Laboratory Method, a simplified version of the scientific method designed for children to use.

Students also conduct an experiment in which they study a small sample of a larger population to make estimates about the population. Your child will collect and organize data, find averages, make and read bar graphs, and make and check predictions.

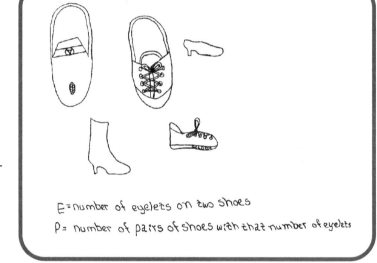

Students draw pictures to show what an experiment is about and what the important variables are.

You can help your child with the work in this unit by:

• Talking about the mathematics you use every day—the measuring you do when you cook or computations you do when you pay the sitter.

• Asking your child to explain the mathematics he or she is doing in school.

• Reviewing the addition and subtraction facts with your child. If your child needs more practice, he or she will be given flash cards and games to use at home.

Sincerely,

_____

Carta al hogar

Poblaciones y muestras

Fecha: _____

Estimado miembro de familia:

Bienvenido a *Math Trailblazers®: A Balanced Mathematics Program Integrating Science and Language Arts.* Durante el año escolar usaremos las matemáticas para resolver muchos tipos de problemas diferentes. A medida que hagamos esto, su hijo/a va a desarrollar habilidades matemáticas necesarias y va a experimentar cómo se usan las matemáticas para resolver problemas de la vida real.

Esta unidad comienza con un estudio breve sobre el número de ojillos en los zapatos de los estudiantes. Esta investigación introduce el método de investigación TIMS, una versión simplificada del método científico diseñada para niños.

Los estudiantes también realizan un experimento en el cual estudian una pequeña muestra de una población más grande para hacer estimaciones sobre la población. Su hijo/a reunirá y organizará datos, hallará promedios, hará y leerá gráficas de barras, y hará y comprobará predicciones.

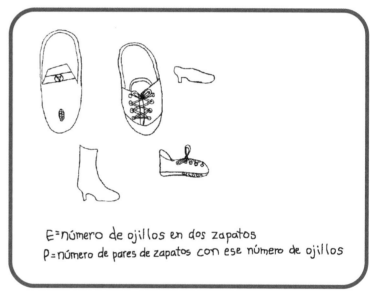

E = número de ojillos en dos zapatos
P = número de pares de zapatos con ese número de ojillos

Los estudiantes hacen dibujos para explicar de qué trata un experimento cuáles son las variables importantes.

Usted puede ayudar a su hijo/a con el trabajo en esta unidad haciendo lo siguiente:

- Hablando de las matemáticas que usa todos los días: las medidas que hace cuando cocina o los cálculos que hace cuando le paga a la niñera.

- Pidiéndole a su hijo/a que le explique las matemáticas que está haciendo en la escuela.

- Repasando los conceptos básicos de suma y resta con su hijo/a. Si su hijo/a necesita más práctica, le daremos tarjetas y juegos para usar en casa.

Atentamente,

_____

Table of Contents

Unit 1
Populations and Samples

Unit 1

Outline
Populations and Samples

Unit Summary

This unit is designed to start the year off right by establishing a positive classroom atmosphere, introducing critical mathematics, and gathering baseline assessment data about students' mathematical abilities.

Students begin the unit with a lab called *Eyelets* that sets a cooperative atmosphere and reviews concepts used in earlier grades. Two activities from fourth grade review finding the median and collecting, organizing, and graphing data in bar graphs. Throughout the unit, students translate between graphs and real-world events. The *Searching the Forest* lab, which will help you gather baseline data on students' mathematical abilities, focuses on populations and samples.

The Adventure Book, *A Matter of Survival,* further explores these concepts. The DPP for this unit will allow you to assess students' fluency with the addition and subtraction facts.

Major Concept Focus

- numerical and categorical variables
- TIMS Laboratory Method
- addition and subtraction fact review
- averages: medians and modes
- interpreting graphs
- bar graphs
- finding the probability of an event
- populations and samples
- *Adventure Book:* populations and samples
- solving problems in more than one way
- choosing appropriate methods to solve problems

Pacing Suggestions

This unit is designed to be completed in nine to twelve days. However, several issues will impact how quickly a class will complete the unit:

- If students have had *Math Trailblazers* in previous grades, use the minimum number of class sessions for each lesson as a guide for lesson planning. If students have not had *Math Trailblazers,* use the maximum number of days as a guide.
- Lesson 2: *Review: Representing Data* is designed for students who did not have *Math Trailblazers* in fourth grade. The material is taken from Unit 1 of fourth grade and prepares students for data collection activities in fifth grade. Omit the lesson if students are already familiar with the content.
- The pacing schedule for the year assumes that mathematics instruction begins on the first day of school and that students receive 60 minutes of mathematics instruction each day. The first lesson is a data collection activity set in a context designed specifically to engage students on the first day of school.
- It is not necessary to stop and make sure students have mastered each skill before moving on to Unit 2, since later units will review and extend the skills and concepts developed in Unit 1. Students will also review skills in the Daily Practice and Problems (in each *Unit Resource Guide*) and Home Practice (in the *Discovery Assignment Book*).

The table below shows the location of resources that provide information on the development of concepts and skills throughout the year.

Resources for Pacing	Location
Curriculum Sequence	In Most Lesson Guides
Unit Scope and Sequence	*Teacher Implementation Guide*
Daily Practice and Problems and Home Practice Scope and Sequence	*Teacher Implementation Guide*
Individual Assessment Record Sheet	*Teacher Implementation Guide*

Assessment Indicators

Use these indicators to assess students on key ideas. Those ideas that can be easily assessed through classroom observation and discussion are listed on the *Observational Assessment Record* that follows the Background section in this unit. For more information regarding assessment, see the Assessment section in the *Teacher Implementation Guide*.

The *Teacher Implementation Guide* contains a set of blackline masters that list the Assessment Indicators from the *Observational Assessment Record* in order. This set is called the *Individual Assessment Record Sheet*. You can use these blackline masters to monitor an individual student's growth over time. The *Individual Assessment Record Sheet* can be included in students' portfolios.

- **A1.** Can students collect, organize, graph, and analyze data?
- **A2.** Can students make and interpret bar graphs?
- **A3.** Can students find the median of a data set?
- **A4.** Do students work well in small groups?
- **A5.** Do students solve problems in more than one way?
- **A6.** Do students demonstrate fluency with the addition and subtraction facts?

Unit Planner

	Lesson Information	Supplies	Copies/Transparencies
Lesson 1 **Eyelets** URG Pages 28–49 SG Pages 2–9 DPP A–F HP Parts 1–2 *Estimated Class Sessions* **3**	**Lab** Students use the TIMS Laboratory Method to carry out a brief study of the number of eyelets in shoes in the classroom. **Math Facts** Use DPP Bits C and E to assess students' fluency with addition facts. Use the Addition and Subtraction Math Facts Review section of the *Facts Resource Guide* with students who need additional facts practice. **Homework** 1. Assign *Questions 1–4* in the Homework section in the *Student Guide*. 2. Assign Parts 1 and 2 of the Home Practice in the *Discovery Assignment Book*. **Assessment** Use the *Pockets at St. Crispin's* Assessment Page found at the end of the Lesson Guide.		• 1 copy of *Pockets at St. Crispin's* URG Page 41 per student • 2 copies of *Centimeter Grid Paper* URG Page 42 per student • 2 copies of *Two-column Data Table* URG Page 43 per student • 1 transparency of *Two-column Data Table* URG Page 43 or laminated data table wall chart or poster-size paper • 1 transparency of *Centimeter Grid Paper* URG Page 42 or laminated graph wall chart or poster-size paper
Lesson 2 **Review: Representing Data** URG Pages 50–75 *Estimated Class Sessions* **2-3**	OPTIONAL LESSON REVIEW FROM GRADE 4 **Optional Activity** This lesson is for students who did not use *Math Trailblazers* last year. The material is taken from Grade 4 Unit 1. It provides experiences with collecting, organizing, and graphing numerical data. **Math Facts** Use the Addition and Subtraction Math Facts Review section of the *Facts Resource Guide* as needed. **Homework** Assign the Homework sections of the *Collecting, Organizing, and Graphing* Activity Pages and the *Finding the Median* Activity Pages. **Assessment** Use the *Observational Assessment Record* and students' *Individual Assessment Record Sheets* to record students' abilities to make bar graphs.	• class-generated data table, Variables and Possible Values, from Lesson 1	• 1 copy of *Collecting, Organizing, and Graphing Data* URG Pages 63–65 per student • 1 copy of *Finding the Median* URG Pages 66–69 per student • 2 copies of *Centimeter Graph Paper* URG Page 70 per student • 1 transparency of *Bar Graph I: What's Wrong Here?* URG Page 61 • 1 transparency of *Bar Graph II: What's Wrong Here?* URG Page 62 • 1 transparency of *Three-column Data Table* URG Page 71 or laminated data table wall chart or poster-size paper • several transparencies of *Two-column Data Table* URG Page 43 or laminated data table wall chart or poster-size paper • 1 transparency of *Centimeter Graph Paper* URG Page 70 or laminated graph wall chart or poster-size paper • 1 copy of *Observational Assessment Record* URG Pages 13–14 to be used throughout this unit • 1 copy of *Individual Assessment Record Sheet* TIG Assessment section per student, to be used throughout the year

	Lesson Information	Supplies	Copies/ Transparencies
Lesson 3 **Analyzing Data** URG Pages 76–89 SG Pages 10–16 DPP G–H HP Part 3 *Estimated Class Sessions* **1**	**Activity** Students analyze graphs and review averages (medians and modes). **Math Facts** Use the Addition and Subtraction Math Facts Review section of the *Facts Resource Guide* as needed. **Homework** 1. Assign the Homework section in the *Student Guide.* 2. Assign Part 3 of the Home Practice in the *Discovery Assignment Book.* **Assessment** Use *Question 1* in the Homework section as an assessment.		
Lesson 4 **A Matter of Survival** URG Pages 90–97 AB Pages 1–12 DPP I–J *Estimated Class Sessions* **1**	**Adventure Book** Betty and her parents sample animal populations in the Amazon rain forest. This story sets the stage for the lab in Lesson 5. **Math Facts** Use the Addition and Subtraction Math Facts Review section of the *Facts Resource Guide* as needed. **Homework** Assign item I from the Daily Practice and Problems.	• a map of South America, optional	
Lesson 5 **Searching the Forest** URG Pages 98–118 SG Pages 17–23 DPP K–P HP Parts 4–5 *Estimated Class Sessions* **3**	**Assessment Lab** Students model sampling an animal population in the forest by sampling a "population" of colored square-inch tiles in a bag. Students add this lab to their collection folders to collect baseline assessment data on their abilities to collect, organize, graph, and analyze data. **Math Facts** 1. Use Bits K and O to assess students' fluency with the subtraction facts. 2. Use the Addition and Subtraction Math Facts Review section of the *Facts Resource Guide* as needed. **Homework** 1. You can use Radio Favorites and Candy Grab in the Homework section of the *Student Guide* for homework during the lab. 2. Assign Parts 4 and 5 of the Home Practice. **Assessment** 1. Use *Jocelyn's Wildflowers* Assessment Page in the *Unit Resource Guide* as a quiz. 2. Evaluate students' labs based on the suggestions in the Assessment section of the Lesson Guide and in the Assessment section in the *Teacher Implementation Guide.*	• colored square-inch tiles, at least 50 in at least 2 colors per student group; more tiles in up to 5 colors is better • 1 brown lunch bag or opaque sack per student group • 1 letter-sized envelope per student group	• 1 copy of *Jocelyn's Wildflowers* URG Page 112 per student • 3 copies of *Centimeter Graph Paper* URG Page 70 per student • 1 copy of *Three-trial Data Table* URG Page 113 per student • 1 copy of *Three-column Data Table* URG Page 71 per student • 1 copy of *Two-column Data Table* URG Page 43 per student • 1 transparency of *Centimeter Graph Paper* URG Page 70, optional • 1 transparency or poster of Student Rubric: *Knowing* TIG, Assessment section, optional

	Lesson Information	Supplies	Copies/Transparencies
	3. Students save their labs in their collection folders.		
Lesson 6 **Practice Problems** URG Pages 119–124 SG Page 24 DPP Q–R HP Part 6 *Estimated Class Sessions* **1**	**Activity** Students solve a variety of multistep problems. **Math Facts** Use the Addition and Subtraction Math Facts Review section of the *Facts Resource Guide* as needed. **Homework** 1. Assign some or all of the problems for homework. 2. Assign Part 6 of the Home Practice.	• 1 calculator per student	

Preparing for Upcoming Lessons

Students will build an abacus in *The Chinese Abacus* in Unit 2 Lesson 4. Begin collecting 12 cm by 24 cm pieces of cardboard, string, and beads or ditali noodles (small noodles found in most grocery stores) to make the abacuses.

Begin collecting pennies. Students will need about 20 pennies per group to complete *Stack Up* in Unit 2 Lesson 9.

Connections

A current list of literature and software connections is available at *www.mathtrailblazers.com*. You can also find information on connections in the *Teacher Implementation Guide* Literature List and Software List sections.

Literature Connections

Suggested Titles

- Bash, Barbara. *Ancient Ones*. Sierra Club, San Francisco, 1994. (Lesson 4)
- George, Jean Craighead. *One Day in the Tropical Rain Forest*. HarperCollins, New York, 1990. (Lesson 4)
- Kipling, Rudyard. *The Jungle Books*. Bantam Books, New York, 2000. (Lesson 4)
- Yolen, Jane. *Welcome to the Green House*. Scholastic, New York, 1994. (Lesson 4)

Software Connections

- *A Field Trip to the Rainforest Deluxe* integrates mathematics with science.
- *Graph Master* allows students to collect data and create their own graphs. (Lesson 5)
- *Math Mysteries: Advanced Whole Numbers* is a series of structured multistep word problems dealing with whole numbers.
- *Math Mysteries: Whole Numbers* is a series of structured word problems dealing with whole numbers.
- *Number Facts Fire Zapper* provides practice in number facts in an arcade-like game.
- *Number Sense and Problem Solving: Puzzle Tanks* develops logical thinking while practicing math facts.
- *Ten Tricky Tiles* provides practice with number facts through engaging puzzles.
- *TinkerPlots* allows students to record, compare, and analyze data in tables and graphs.

Teaching All Math Trailblazers Students

Math Trailblazers lessons are designed for students with a wide range of abilities. The lessons are flexible and do not require significant adaptation for diverse learning styles or academic levels. However, when needed, lessons can be tailored to allow students to engage their abilities to the greatest extent possible while building knowledge and skills.

The lessons in *Math Trailblazers* foster the kind of environment recommended by the National Council of Teachers of Mathematics *Principles and Standards for School Mathematics,* an environment that encourages students to explore, take risks, share failures and successes, and question one another. The Council asserts that in such supportive environments, students develop the confidence they need to explore problems and the ability to make adjustments in their problem-solving strategies.

Early in the year, lessons focus on gathering baseline information about students' mathematical knowledge. These lessons help to establish a classroom environment in which the mathematical content, the process in which students work with the content, and the product of students' work can be examined in a variety of ways. Continually assessing your student's growing knowledge as they explore the variety of content areas in *Math Trailblazers* will help you understand the types of accommodations different children may need throughout the year.

To assist you in meeting the needs of all students in your classroom, this section contains information about some of the features in the curriculum that allow all students access to mathematics. For additional information, see the Teaching the *Math Trailblazers* Student: Meeting Individual Needs section in the *Teacher Implementation Guide.* See the *Math Trailblazers* Classroom section in the *Teacher implementation Guide* for more information on establishing and maintaining a positive, engaging, and challenging classroom environment for students of all abilities.

Differentiation Opportunities in this Unit

Games

Use games to promote or extend understanding of math concepts and to practice skills with children who need more practice.

- DPP item N *Play Digits Game* from Lesson 5 *Searching the Forest*
- DPP item P *Play Digits Game Again* from Lesson 5 *Searching the Forest*

Laboratory Experiments

Laboratory experiments enable students to solve problems using a variety of representations including pictures, tables, graphs, and symbols. Teachers can assign or adapt parts of the analysis according to the student's ability. The following lessons have a lab:

- Lesson 1 *Eyelets*
- Lesson 5 *Searching the Forest*

Journal Prompts

Journal prompts provide opportunities for students to explain and reflect on mathematical problems. They can help both students who need practice explaining their ideas and students who benefit from answering higher order questions. Students with various learning styles can express themselves using pictures, words, and sentences. Teachers can alter journal prompts to suit students' ability levels. The following lessons contain a journal prompt:

- Lesson 1 *Eyelets*
- Lesson 2 *Review: Representing Data*
- Lesson 3 *Analyzing Data*
- Lesson 5 *Searching the Forest*

DPP Challenges

DPP Challenges are items from the Daily Practice and Problems that usually take more than fifteen minutes to complete. These problems are more thought-provoking and can be used to stretch students' problem-solving skills. The following lessons have a DPP Challenge in them:

- DPP Challenge D from Lesson 1 *Eyelets*
- DPP Challenge J from Lesson 4 *A Matter of Survival*

Extensions

Use extensions to enrich lessons. Many extensions provide opportunities to further involve or challenge students of all abilities.

Take a moment to review the extensions prior to beginning this unit. Some extensions may require additional preparation and planning. The following lessons contain extensions:

- Lesson 1 *Eyelets*
- Lesson 2 *Review: Representing Data*
- Lesson 3 *Analyzing Data*
- Lesson 4 *A Matter of Survival*
- Lesson 5 *Searching the Forest*

Background
Populations and Samples

During the first days of school, routines and expectations are established that make a big difference in how pleasant and productive your class will be all year. The lessons in this unit are designed to help you start the year right.

The principal aims of this unit are to:

- establish a positive classroom atmosphere;
- introduce critical mathematics and science content; and
- gather baseline assessment data on students' mathematical knowledge.

The main context for this work is studying populations ranging from monkeys in the Amazon rain forest to colored tiles in a brown paper sack to the number of eyelets on students' shoes.

Positive Classroom Atmosphere and Beliefs about Mathematics

A major goal at the beginning of the school year is to support certain beliefs about mathematics. These include:

- problems can be solved in more than one way;
- various methods should yield the same solution;
- solution methods should be explained, discussed, compared, and contrasted;
- some problems are hard and may require more than a few minutes to solve;
- it is acceptable to make mistakes;
- mathematics makes sense;
- often people work alone in mathematics, but they also often work together;
- mathematics relates to life outside school; and
- mathematics is enjoyable.

The activities in this unit are designed to further these beliefs, but since many of them are not widely held, be explicit about encouraging them. The unit also helps establish a classroom atmosphere that promotes working cooperatively and using manipulatives appropriately.

Mathematics and Science Content

The most important mathematics and science content in this unit can be summed up in two words: method and variables. Both concepts are discussed briefly here. For a more detailed discussion, see the TIMS Tutor: *The TIMS Laboratory Method* in the *Teacher Implementation Guide*.

Method

One principal goal of this unit is to review (or introduce) the TIMS Laboratory Method, a simplified version of the scientific method. The TIMS Laboratory Method has four phases: beginning the investigation, collecting and organizing data, graphing the data, and analyzing the results.

We eventually want students to apply the TIMS Laboratory Method on their own, and if your fifth graders had *Math Trailblazers* in earlier grades, you should be able to "turn them loose" as early as this first unit. Students who have not had *Math Trailblazers* before will need more guidance, especially in the beginning. One of your more difficult instructional decisions will be how much guidance to give—how to balance imitation and autonomy. More imitation will make for more orderly lessons, an important consideration in the beginning of the year. On the other hand, too much imitation can undermine student autonomy and can foster wrong impressions about what mathematics and science are. In the long run what really matters is what students can do on their own, without their teacher's help.

The first lab, *Eyelets,* will accommodate a range of approaches from teacher-directed to open-ended. In the main part of the lab you can be as directive as you think appropriate, especially since there is one data set for the whole class rather than a separate data set for each group.

The second lab, *Searching the Forest,* has been designated as a baseline assessment lab so you can use it as a starting point for measuring growth in students' mathematical knowledge throughout the year. The lab demands more student autonomy since student groups gather their own data. Imitation is still important, but now every group's data is different. This means that only methods, not results, can be imitated.

A great advantage of the TIMS Laboratory Method, with its multiple representations of mathematical ideas, is that it allows each student to work at his or her own level. Problems set in the rich context of a TIMS lab can often be solved by several methods, through mathematical reasoning, analysis of the graph or data tables, or even direct application of the laboratory apparatus. This allows a wide range of students to be accommodated by a single lesson. Discussing their solution methods also helps students develop their communication skills at the same time they are learning from one another.

Variables

Variables are attributes or quantities that change or vary in an experiment. They are basic to mathematics and science. Students should see the experiments as investigations about relationships between variables. *Eyelets* can be seen as a study of how many pairs of shoes (P) there are with certain numbers of eyelets (E); *Searching the Forest* is a study of the number of tiles (N) of each color (C).

Several basic procedures for handling variables are involved in this unit:

- identifying the two main variables in an experiment;
- distinguishing between variables and values (Possible values of the variable color are red, green, blue, etc. Possible values of the variable number of eyelets are 4, 8, 12, etc.);
- denoting variables by symbols (C for color, E for number of eyelets);
- labeling data table columns and graph axes with variable names.

For most students who had *Math Trailblazers* before, this will be familiar.

Averages

An **average** is a single value that represents a set of numbers. Although the mean is the most commonly used average in everyday activities, students learn to use three kinds of averages (mean, median, and mode) as part of their collection and analysis of data. Use of the mean is reviewed in Unit 4. In this unit, the mode is introduced in Lessons 1 and 2 and the median is reviewed in Lessons 2 and 3. For more information on averages and how they are used, see the Content Note in Lesson 3 and the TIMS Tutor: *Averages* in the *Teacher Implementation Guide*.

Context: Populations and Samples

The study of populations is the context for much of this work with the TIMS Laboratory Method, variables, beliefs, and classroom climate. A **population** is a group of persons or things used as a base in statistical measurement. Thus, we can talk about the population of Chicago or Paducah, but we can also talk about the population of leaves on the General Sherman giant sequoia tree, the population of deer in a state, or even the population of widgets made by U.S. Widget in 1956.

Sometimes an entire population is small enough and well-defined enough for each individual to be counted or measured: the population of giant pandas in U.S. zoos, for example, can be counted or measured directly. More often, however, it is impossible, impractical, or unnecessary to count or measure an entire population: the population of giant pandas in the wilds of western China, for example, cannot be counted exactly. However, even when an entire population cannot be studied directly, there is often a way to gather useful information about it—sampling.

Samples

A **sample** is a part or subset of a population. If you pull five leaves from a tree, you have a sample from the population of leaves on that tree; if you interview ten people leaving a polling place, then you have sampled the voting population at that location; if you pull a handful from a bowl of jellybeans, then you have sampled the jellybean population of that bowl. By studying a sample, one can often draw probable conclusions about the underlying population: If three of five oak leaves show evidence of a blight, then it's likely the tree has a problem; if eight of ten voters state that they voted for thc incumbent, then that candidate is probably in good shape; if half the handful of jellybeans is red, then it's a good bet that about half the beans in the bowl are red, as well.

Sampling is worth studying both for its applications—public opinion polling, statistical process control, wildlife population estimation, indeed, much scientific research in general. It is also worth studying the interesting mathematics it requires: variables, classification, probability, mathematical reasoning, and statistics. *Math Trailblazers* students begin studying populations and sampling in first grade when they pull handfuls of colored objects from grab bags. Population studies in the form of grab bags, frequency distributions, and classification labs are included in every later grade. The two labs in this unit are part of this series. The breadth and power of the mathematics of such population studies make a rich beginning for what we hope will be a most productive school year.

Review and Practice

Every unit includes a section in the *Unit Resource Guide* called the Daily Practice and Problems (DPP). This set of short exercises provides distributed practice in computation and a structure for the review of the math facts. It also develops other concepts and skills such as number sense, mental math, telling time, and working with money. Lastly, the items in the DPP review topics from earlier units. In each unit there is a Lesson Guide for the DPP. This guide categorizes the items so you can locate a problem that reviews a certain concept or skill.

Every unit includes a section in the *Discovery Assignment Book* called Home Practice. It is a series of problems that supplement the homework included in the lessons. The Home Practice distributes skill practice throughout the units and reviews concepts studied in previous units. The Homework and Practice section in each Lesson Guide may suggest the appropriate parts of the Home Practice to assign with the lesson.

For more information on the Home Practice or the Daily Practice and Problems, see the *Daily Practice*

and Problems and Home Practice Guide in the *Teacher Implementation Guide*. The *Teacher Implementation Guide* also contains a Scope and Sequence for the Daily Practice and Problems, which sorts items by unit as well as by topic. The scope and sequence can serve as a content map for individual DPP items.

This unit's content will be revisited in different contexts many times throughout the year. Thus, it is not necessary to expect mastery of each concept or skill at this juncture. Rather, move through the activities relatively quickly and use the early units to determine where your students need the most work.

Baseline Assessment

Each student is valued for the knowledge and skills he or she brings to the classroom. At the same time we expect each student to make significant gains during the year. This unit will provide baseline data on the knowledge your students possess at the beginning of the school year. Students will begin placing materials in their collection folders. In Unit 2, students will create formal assessment portfolios that will be used to assess progress in mathematics over the course of the school year. Each student will add to his or her portfolio throughout the year. See the TIMS Tutor: *Portfolios* for information on the use of assessment portfolios. Also, see the *Assessment* section in the *Teacher Implementation Guide* for more information about the overall assessment program in fifth grade.

One tool that helps students reflect on their work is a set of three TIMS Student Rubrics. The rubrics provide guides for students about what to look for in outstanding work. Three areas—"Knowing," "Solving," and "Telling"—are covered. The areas correspond to a scoring guide—the *TIMS Multidimensional Rubric*—that you can use to assess students' work.

As part of this unit, students are introduced to the *Knowing* Student Rubric. They use the rubric as a guide as they reason through the mathematics they explore. In Unit 2, students will be introduced to the other two dimensions, the *Telling* and the *Solving* dimensions. For more information about the *TIMS Multidimensional Rubric*, see the *Teacher Implementation Guide*.

Resources

The following books and articles about assessment were written with classroom teachers in mind:

- Mathematics Sciences Education Board. *Measuring Up: Prototypes for Mathematics Assessment*. National Academy Press, Washington, DC, 1993.

- Payne, J.N. (Ed.) *Mathematics for the Young Child*. National Council of Teachers of Mathematics, Reston, VA, 1990.

- *Principles and Standards for School Mathematics*. National Council of Teachers of Mathematics, Reston, VA, 2000.

- Stenmark, J.K. (Ed.) *Mathematics Assessment: Myths, Models, Good Questions, and Practical Suggestions*. National Council of Teachers of Mathematics, Reston, VA, 1991.

- Webb, N.L. (Ed.) *Assessment in the Mathematics Classroom*. National Council of Teachers of Mathematics, Reston, VA, 1993.

- Zawojewski, Judith S. "Polishing a Data Task: Seeking Better Assessment" in *Teaching Children Mathematics*. Volume 2, Number 6, National Council of Teachers of Mathematics, Reston, VA, February 1996.

Observational Assessment Record

You may use the following questions to assess your students' progress. You may wish to assess additional content.

A1 Can students collect, organize, graph, and analyze data?

A2 Can students make and interpret bar graphs?

A3 Can students find the median of a data set?

A4 Do students work well in small groups?

A5 Do students solve problems in more than one way?

A6 Do students demonstrate fluency with the addition and subtraction facts?

A7 _____

Name	A1	A2	A3	A4	A5	A6	A7	Comments
1.								
2.								
3.								
4.								
5.								
6.								
7.								
8.								
9.								
10.								
11.								
12.								
13.								

Name	A1	A2	A3	A4	A5	A6	A7	Comments
14.								
15.								
16.								
17.								
18.								
19.								
20.								
21.								
22.								
23.								
24.								
25.								
26.								
27.								
28.								
29.								
30.								
31.								
32.								

Unit 1

Daily Practice and Problems
Populations and Samples

A DPP Menu for Unit 1

Two Daily Practice and Problems (DPP) items are included for each class session listed in the Unit Outline. A scope and sequence chart for the DPP is in the *Teacher Implementation Guide*.

Icons in the Teacher Notes column designate the subject matter of each DPP item. The first item in each class session is always a Bit and the second is either a Task or Challenge. Each item falls into one or more of the categories listed below. A menu of the DPP items for Unit 1 follows.

N Number Sense	✖ Computation	🕐 Time	⬡ Geometry
B, D, I, L–N, P, Q	A, C, E, G, K–P, R		
5×7 Math Facts	$ Money	⚖ Measurement	▨ Data
B, C, E, K, O	G, J		D, F, H, M, Q

The DPP items found at the beginning of each unit are short exercises that:

- provide distributed practice in computation and a structure for systematic review of the basic math facts;

- develop concepts and skills such as number sense, mental math, telling time, and working with money throughout the year; and

- review topics from earlier units, presenting concepts in new contexts and linking ideas from unit to unit.

There are three types of items: Bits, Tasks, and Challenges. Most are written so that they can be quickly copied onto the board.

- Bits are short and should take no more than five or ten minutes to complete. They often provide practice with a skill or the basic math facts. We recommend that students complete one Bit for each class session.

- Tasks take ten or fifteen minutes to complete and in some instances expand on a topic presented in the previous Bit.

- Challenges usually take longer than fifteen minutes to complete and the problems are more thought-provoking. They can be used to stretch students' problem-solving skills.

Tasks or Challenges may be appropriate as the "Problem of the Day," homework, assessment, or as enrichment activities for students who need a challenge.

Refer to the *Daily Practice and Problems and Home Practice Guide* in the *Teacher Implementation Guide* for further information on the DPP. It includes information on how and when to use the DPP. A Scope and Sequence Chart for the Daily Practice and Problems for the year can be found in the *Teacher Implementation Guide*.

Review and Assessment of Math Facts

Students using *Math Trailblazers* are expected to demonstrate fluency with each of the four groups of math facts (addition, subtraction, multiplication, and division) according to the following timetable:

- by the end of second grade: addition and subtraction facts
- by the end of third grade: multiplication facts
- by the end of fourth grade: division facts
- during fifth grade: review of multiplication and division facts

Some DPP items for the first unit of fifth grade review the addition and subtraction facts. DPP items for Unit 2 begin a systematic review of the multiplication and division facts.

Baseline Assessment

DPP items C, E, K, and O provide an opportunity for you to assess students informally on the addition and subtraction facts. By using these items, you can determine which students need extra practice. Those who can find answers to the problems in these items quickly and efficiently will continue to practice the addition and subtraction facts throughout the year as they engage in labs, activities, and games, and as they solve problems in the DPP. However, for those students who need extra practice, use the *Addition and Subtraction Math Facts Review* section in the *Facts Resource Guide*. In this section are diagnostic tests you can use to assess students more formally and to determine which specific facts students need to practice. Administer the diagnostic tests over a period of time. Then, encourage students to use the suggested activities and games to practice the facts they need to learn.

Distributed Practice

Students should use the suggested activities, games, and flash cards in the *Addition and Subtraction Math Facts Review* at home with family members,

concentrating on one small group of facts at a time. Practicing small groups of facts often (for short periods of time) is more effective than practicing many facts less often (for long periods of time). While students practice the addition and subtraction facts at home, encourage them to use strategies, calculators, and printed addition and subtraction tables in class as they solve problems. These tools allow students to continue to develop number sense and work on interesting problems and experiments while they are learning the facts. In this way, students who need extra practice are not prevented from learning more complex mathematics because they do not know all the math facts.

Ongoing Assessment

The informal assessments provided in the DPP as well as the short diagnostic tests in the *Addition and Subtraction Math Facts Review* section do not include all the addition and subtraction facts. These short assessments are less threatening and as effective as longer tests. Tests of all the facts for any operation have a very limited role. Since we rarely, if ever, need to recall 100 facts at one time in the real world, overemphasizing tests of all the facts reinforces the notion that math is nothing more than rote memorization and has no connection to the real world. Tests that include a small number of facts give teachers, students, and parents the information needed to continue learning and practicing the facts efficiently. The goal of the math facts assessment program is to determine the degree to which students can find answers to fact problems quickly and accurately and whether they can retain this skill over time. For more information about the distribution of math fact practice and the assessment of the math facts, see the *Facts Resource Guide,* the TIMS Tutor: *Math Facts,* and the *Assessment* section in the *Teacher Implementation Guide*.

The *Addition and Subtraction Math Facts Review* section also includes a second form of each of the five diagnostic tests. Administer these tests over a period of time after students are given the opportunity to use some of the items in the *Addition and Subtraction Math Facts Review*.

Students may solve the items individually, in groups, or as a class. The items may also be assigned for homework. The DPPs are also available on the Teacher Resource CD.

Student Questions	Teacher Notes

A Adding and Subtracting

Do these problems in your head.

A. $34 + 5 =$

B. $50 + 45 =$

C. $89 + 3 =$

D. $104 - 5 =$

E. $128 + 20 =$

F. $210 + 56 =$

G. $205 - 105 =$

H. $83 - 40 =$

I. $919 - 800 =$

TIMS Bit

Discuss students' strategies.

A. 39	B. 95
C. 92	D. 99
E. 148	F. 266
G. 100	H. 43
I. 119	

B Who Am I?

I am greater than $5 + 6$ but less than $12 + 8$.

I am an even number.

If you skip count by 3s, you'll say me.

I am not 18.

Write a riddle of your own. Exchange it with a friend.

TIMS Task

12

Addition Review 1

Solve the following using paper and pencil only.

A.	64 +81	B.	43 +94	C.	85 +82
D.	92 +57	E.	81 +93	F.	60 +96
G.	74 +85	H.	92 +92	I.	46 +73
J.	50 +58	K.	32 +82	L.	69 +60

TIMS Bit

Since these addition problems do not involve any regrouping, they can be used to assess students' fluency with the addition facts. These problems, along with those in DPP item E, include most of the basic addition facts students should know. If some students need addition fact practice, assign them activities, games, and flash cards from the *Addition and Subtraction Math Facts Review* in the *Facts Resource Guide*.

A.	145	B.	137
C.	167	D.	149
E.	174	F.	156
G.	159	H.	184
I.	119	J.	108
K.	114	L.	129

 How Many?

1. Estimate the number of times you blink during the school day.

2. Estimate the number of videos your local video store displays.

3. Estimate the number of cars that drive through a particular intersection in your neighborhood in one day.

TIMS Challenge

Answers will vary. One way to determine the answer to this type of question is to take a sample of data and then use multiplication of convenient numbers to find a good estimate for the total.

Addition Review 2

Solve the following using paper and pencil only.

A.　75
　 +33

B.　72
　 +94

C.　54
　 +84

D.　53
　 +72

E.　88
　 +21

F.　63
　 +73

G.　46
　 +82

H.　50
　 +60

I.　27
　 +90

J.　31
　 +91

K.　47
　 +61

L.　71
　 +76

TIMS Bit

Like the problems in DPP item C, these addition problems do not involve any regrouping. Thus they can be used to assess students' fluency with the addition facts. These problems, along with those in DPP item C, include most of the basic addition facts students should know. If some students need addition fact practice, assign them activities, games, and flash cards from the *Addition and Subtraction Math Facts Review* in the *Facts Resource Guide*.

A.	108	B.	166
C.	138	D.	125
E.	109	F.	136
G.	128	H.	110
I.	117	J.	122
K.	108	L.	147

F Variables and Values

Below is a list of variables Mr. Moreno's class wants to study to get to know one another.

A. Day of the week you were born.

B. Time of day you were born.

C. Month you were born.

D. Number of brothers and sisters.

E. Favorite season of the year.

F. Favorite hobby.

G. Number of stuffed animals in your room.

1. Decide if each variable is numerical or categorical.

2. Name three possible values for each variable.

TIMS Task

A. Categorical: Sunday, Monday, Tuesday, etc.

B. Numerical: 8:00 A.M., 11:30 A.M., 10:02 P.M., etc.

C. Categorical: January, February, March, etc.

D. Numerical: 0, 1, 2, 3, etc.

E. Categorical: winter, spring, summer, and fall

F. Categorical: sports, reading, in-line skating, etc.

G. Numerical: 0, 1, 2, 3, etc.

G Purchasing Shoes

Alexander is purchasing a pair of shoes for $23.95 and two new pairs of socks at $1.25 each.

1. How much is Alexander's purchase without tax?

2. With tax, Alexander owes the sales clerk $28.30. About how much was the tax?

3. If Alexander gives the clerk $30.00, how much change should he receive?

TIMS Bit

Encourage students to find ways to do these problems in their heads. Discuss and compare students' problem-solving strategies.

1. $26.45

2. about $2

3. $1.70

What's for Lunch?

Mr. Moreno's class went on a field trip to the museum. They went to lunch in the museum cafeteria. Shannon collected the following data about what her classmates ate for lunch.

Type of Food	Number of Students
Tacos	3
Pizza	10
Hamburgers	15
Chicken	2

1. Make a bar graph of Shannon's data on graph paper.

2. What variable did you graph on the horizontal axis?

3. What variable did you graph on the vertical axis?

4. Identify each variable as categorical or numerical.

5. What are some questions you could answer using the graph?

TIMS Task

1. *Centimeter Graph Paper* is located in Lesson 2.

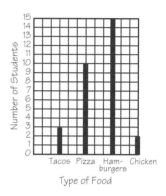

2. Type of food

3. Number of students

4. Type of food is categorical. Number of students is numerical.

5. Sample questions are: What was the most commonly chosen food? How many more people chose hamburgers than pizza?

Skip Counting

1. List the multiples of 2 from 2 to 30. (Skip count by 2s from 2 to 30.)

2. List the multiples of 4 from 4 to 40.

3. List the multiples of 5 from 5 to 50.

4. List the multiples of 10 from 10 to 200.

TIMS Bit

In the lab *Eyelets* in Lesson 1, the values for the number of eyelets on pairs of shoes are all multiples of 4.

In the lab *Searching the Forest* in Lesson 5, students must create a population of square-inch tiles in a bag. The number of tiles of each color must be a multiple of 10. You may use this bit to review multiples. This bit can be completed orally.

J **Counting Pennies**

Marianne counted a jug of pennies her family collected. She emptied the jug by taking ten pennies out at a time. She made a tally mark for every ten pennies. When she was finished, she had 176 tally marks.

1. How many pennies does she have?

2. How much money does Marianne have? Give your answer in dollars and cents.

3. If the pennies were exchanged for nickels, how many nickels would she have?

4. If the pennies were exchanged for dimes, how many dimes would she have?

5. If the pennies were exchanged for quarters, how many quarters would she have?

TIMS Challenge

1. 1760 pennies
2. $17.60
3. 352 nickels
4. 176 dimes
5. 70 quarters and 1 dime, 10 pennies, or 2 nickels

Subtraction Review 1

Solve the following using paper and pencil only.

A.	1462	B.	1030	C.	1176
	− 750		− 810		− 842

D.	1096	E.	1067	F.	1192
	− 435		− 532		− 962

G.	1255	H.	1685	I.	1234
	− 741		− 941		− 632

J.	1715	K.	1483	L.	1597
	− 902		− 851		− 975

TIMS Bit

Use this item and item O as inventory tests for subtraction fact recall. No regrouping is involved in any of the problems. If some students need practice with the subtraction facts, assign them activities, games, and flash cards from the *Addition and Subtraction Math Facts Review* in the *Facts Resource Guide.*

A. 712	B. 220
C. 334	D. 661
E. 535	F. 230
G. 514	H. 744
I. 602	J. 813
K. 632	L. 622

 Mental Powers

Do the following problems in your head. Be ready to share your strategies with the class.

A. $13 + 27 =$ B. $26 + 14 =$

C. $40 − 15 =$ D. $50 − 26 =$

E. $100 − 27 =$ F. $88 − 58 =$

G. $62 + 66 =$ H. $99 − 25 =$

I. $250 + 625 =$ J. $849 − 550 =$

K. $321 + 421 =$ L. $2378 + 6322 =$

M. $1000 − 478 =$ N. $8910 + 8090 =$

TIMS Task

A. 40	B. 40
C. 25	D. 24
E. 73	F. 30
G. 128	H. 74
I. 875	J. 299
K. 742	L. 8700
M. 522	N. 17,000

Medians

Lin, Irma, Jackie, Arti, and Jessie sold cookies for their girls' club. The following data shows the number of boxes each girl sold.

Student	Number of Boxes Sold
Lin	154 boxes
Irma	78 boxes
Arti	110 boxes
Jackie	100 boxes
Jessie	45 boxes

1. What is the median number of boxes sold?

2. How many more boxes did Lin sell than Jessie?

3. Did Irma and Jessie together sell more or less than Arti?

4. About how many boxes did the five girls sell altogether?

TIMS Bit

1. 100 boxes

2. 109 boxes

3. more

4. About 500 boxes. Answers will vary based on students' strategies. Discuss students' strategies. Which strategies are more efficient?

Play *Digits Game*

Draw boxes like these on your paper.

$$\boxed{}\ \boxed{}$$
$$+\ \boxed{}\ \boxed{}$$
$$\overline{}$$

Your teacher or classmate will choose one card at a time from a set of cards with the digits 0–9. The cards will not be returned to the deck. As the digits are chosen, place them in the boxes. Try to find the largest sum. Remember that each digit will be read only once. Once you place a digit, it cannot be moved.

TIMS Task

Students begin the game by drawing the boxes on their papers. The teacher chooses a digit at random from a set of *Digit Cards 0–9*. As an alternative, you can use a deck of playing cards. The ace can stand for 1 and the joker or a face card for zero.) Students place the selected digit in one of the boxes to try to get the largest sum. Once a digit is placed, it can't be moved. Then the teacher chooses a second digit without replacing the first. Play continues until the teacher has read enough digits. The player with the largest sum wins.

 Subtraction Review 2

Solve the following using paper and pencil.

A. $\begin{array}{r} 1079 \\ -\ \ 772 \\ \hline \end{array}$ B. $\begin{array}{r} 1353 \\ -\ \ 852 \\ \hline \end{array}$ C. $\begin{array}{r} 1669 \\ -\ \ 845 \\ \hline \end{array}$

D. $\begin{array}{r} 1397 \\ -\ \ 901 \\ \hline \end{array}$ E. $\begin{array}{r} 1265 \\ -\ \ 963 \\ \hline \end{array}$ F. $\begin{array}{r} 1478 \\ -\ \ 936 \\ \hline \end{array}$

G. $\begin{array}{r} 1887 \\ -\ \ 926 \\ \hline \end{array}$ H. $\begin{array}{r} 1291 \\ -\ \ 881 \\ \hline \end{array}$ I. $\begin{array}{r} 1198 \\ -\ \ 943 \\ \hline \end{array}$

J. $\begin{array}{r} 1548 \\ -\ \ 837 \\ \hline \end{array}$ K. $\begin{array}{r} 1379 \\ -\ \ 657 \\ \hline \end{array}$ L. $\begin{array}{r} 1184 \\ -\ \ 784 \\ \hline \end{array}$

TIMS Bit

Use this item and item K as inventory tests for subtraction fact recall. No regrouping is involved in any of the problems. If some students need practice, assign them activities, games, and flash cards from the *Addition and Subtraction Math Facts Review* in the *Facts Resource Guide*.

A. 307	B. 501
C. 824	D. 496
E. 302	F. 542
G. 961	H. 410
I. 255	J. 711
K. 722	L. 400

P Play _Digits Game_ Again

Draw boxes like these on your paper.

☐ ☐ ☐

— ☐ ☐

_____

Your teacher or classmate will choose four digits, one at a time, from a set of cards. As each digit is read, place it in one of the boxes. Try to find the largest difference. Remember each digit will be read only once. Once you place a digit, it cannot be moved.

TIMS Task

The game is played as described in item N. This time have students place the digits in the boxes to try to get the largest difference. The player with the largest difference wins. Discuss strategies for placing digits in the boxes.

Q Median Height

1. Find the median height of the Presidents listed below.

2. Find the median weight of the Presidents listed below.

President	Height	Weight
Dwight Eisenhower	5 ft 10 in	180 lbs
John Kennedy	6 ft	175 lbs
Lyndon Johnson	6 ft 3 in	210 lbs
Richard Nixon	5 ft 11 in	175 lbs
Gerald Ford	6 ft	200 lbs
Jimmy Carter	5 ft 9 in	175 lbs
Ronald Reagan	6 ft 1in	185 lbs
George H. W. Bush	6 ft 2 in	195 lbs

TIMS Bit

1. 6 ft
2. $182\frac{1}{2}$ lbs

Addition and Subtraction

Solve the following in your head or using paper and pencil. Estimate to make sure your answers are reasonable.

A. $65 + 79 =$

B. $460 - 183 =$

C. $783 - 594 =$

D. $1089 - 437 =$

E. $2378 + 587 =$

F. $9045 + 2985 =$

TIMS Task

A. 144   B. 277

C. 189   D. 652

E. 2965   F. 12,030

Lesson 1

Eyelets

Estimated Class Sessions

3

Lesson Overview

Students use the TIMS Laboratory Method to carry out a brief study of the number of eyelets in shoes in the classroom.

Key Content

- Collecting, organizing, graphing, and analyzing data.
- Making and interpreting bar graphs.
- Connecting mathematics and science to real-world situations.
- Establishing social norms for cooperation and discourse.
- Promoting the following beliefs:
  1. Problems can be solved by more than one method;
  2. Different methods should yield solutions that agree; and
  3. Mathematics can be relevant and enjoyable.

Key Vocabulary

- categorical variable
- data
- mode
- numerical variable
- values
- variable

Math Facts

Use DPP Bits C and E to assess students' fluency with addition facts. Use the Addition and Subtraction Math Facts Review section of the *Facts Resource Guide* with students who need additional facts practice.

Homework

1. Assign *Questions 1–4* in the Homework section in the *Student Guide*.
2. Assign Parts 1 and 2 of the Home Practice in the *Discovery Assignment Book*.

Assessment

Use the *Pockets at St. Crispin's* Assessment Page found at the end of the Lesson Guide.

Curriculum Sequence

Before This Unit

Variables and Values

Throughout first, second, third, and fourth grades, students using *Math Trailblazers* identified variables and their values in experiments and activities. (See Lessons 1, 2, and 5 of Unit 1 in Grade 4 for examples. Numerical and categorical variables were introduced in Unit 1 Lesson 2 of fourth grade.)

Bar Graphs

Since kindergarten, students have displayed and interpreted data in bar graphs. For example, students reviewed bar graphing in Grade 4 Unit 1 Lessons 1 and 2. In Unit 13 of fourth grade, they used bar graphs to display and analyze data gathered in a survey on the number of hours of television students watch each week.

After This Unit

Variables and Values

The concept of variables is an important theme in fifth grade. Students will have many opportunities to continue to develop this concept. See the labs *Distance vs. Time* in Unit 3 and *Spreading Out* in Unit 4 for examples.

Bar Graphs

In fifth grade, students will continue to use bar graphs to display and analyze data. Lesson 2 of this unit is an optional lesson that uses material from fourth grade to review bar graphing. In particular, they will use bar graphs in their study of probability and statistics in Units 7 and 8.

Materials List

Supplies and Copies

Student	Teacher
Supplies for Each Student	**Supplies**
Copies • 1 copy of *Pockets at St. Crispin's* per student (*Unit Resource Guide* Page 41) • 2 copies of *Centimeter Grid Paper* per student (*Unit Resource Guide* Page 42) • 2 copies of *Two-column Data Table* per student (*Unit Resource Guide* Page 43) **TIMS Tip** Students complete two data tables in this lesson. They can use copies of the *Two-column Data Table* or draw their own tables.	**Copies/Transparencies** • 1 transparency of *Two-column Data Table* or laminated data table wall chart or poster-size paper (*Unit Resource Guide* Page 43) • 1 transparency of *Centimeter Grid Paper* or laminated graph wall chart or poster-size paper (*Unit Resource Guide* Page 42)

All blackline masters including assessment, transparency, and DPP masters are also on the Teacher Resource CD.

Student Books
Eyelets (*Student Guide* Pages 2–9)

Daily Practice and Problems and Home Practice
DPP items A–F (*Unit Resource Guide* Pages 17–20)
Home Practice Parts 1–2 (*Discovery Assignment Book* Page 3)

Note: Classrooms whose pacing differs significantly from the suggested pacing of the units should use the Math Facts Calendar in Section 4 of the *Facts Resource Guide* to ensure students receive the complete math facts program.

Daily Practice and Problems

Suggestions for using the DPPs are on pages 38–39.

A. Bit: Adding and Subtracting (URG p. 17)

Do these problems in your head.

A. 34 + 5 =	B. 50 + 45 =
C. 89 + 3 =	D. 104 − 5 =
E. 128 + 20 =	F. 210 + 56 =
G. 205 − 105 =	H. 83 − 40 =
I. 919 − 800 =	

B. Task: Who Am I? (URG p. 17)

I am greater than 5 + 6 but less than 12 + 8.

I am an even number.

If you skip count by 3s, you'll say me.

I am not 18.

Write a riddle of your own. Exchange it with a friend.

C. Bit: Addition Review 1 (URG p. 18)

Solve the following using paper and pencil only.

A. 64 + 81	B. 43 + 94	C. 85 + 82
D. 92 + 57	E. 81 + 93	F. 60 + 96
G. 74 + 85	H. 92 + 92	I. 46 + 73
J. 50 + 58	K. 32 + 82	L. 69 + 60

D. Challenge: How Many? (URG p. 18)

1. Estimate the number of times you blink during the school day.

2. Estimate the number of videos your local video store displays.

3. Estimate the number of cars that drive through a particular intersection in your neighborhood in one day.

E. Bit: Addition Review 2 (URG p. 19)

Solve the following using paper and pencil only.

A. 75 + 33	B. 72 + 94	C. 54 + 84
D. 53 + 72	E. 88 + 21	F. 63 + 73
G. 46 + 82	H. 50 + 60	I. 27 + 90
J. 31 + 91	K. 47 + 61	L. 71 + 76

F. Task: Variables and Values (URG p. 20)

Below is a list of variables Mr. Moreno's class wants to study to get to know one another.

A. Day of the week you were born.
B. Time of day you were born.
C. Month you were born.
D. Number of brothers and sisters.
E. Favorite season of the year.
F. Favorite hobby.
G. Number of stuffed animals in your room.

1. Decide if each variable is numerical or categorical.

2. Name three possible values for each variable.

Eyelets

Slip-ons and Sneakers

"I'm not sure those sneakers go with that outfit, Blanca," Mrs. Campos said. "Why don't you wear your slip-ons? I think that would look pretty."

"I hate those slip-ons, Mama," answered Blanca. "Nobody wears shoes like that anymore. Don't you want me to look stylish for my first day of fifth grade?"

"Of course I want you to look nice," Mrs. Campos answered. "That's no problem—you're a beautiful girl. But those sneakers . . ."

"Trust me, Mom," interrupted Blanca. "This look is cool."

Later, at school, Blanca met her friend Irma. "¡Hola! Irma. Guess what? My mom wanted me to wear slip-ons for the first day of school. She said sneakers don't go with my outfit."

"Oh, no!" said Irma. "How'd you convince her to let you wear them?"

"I told her to trust me, and she did—for today," said Blanca. "But I'm afraid she'll make me wear those ugly shoes sooner or later. How can I convince her that nobody wears slip-ons anymore?"

"I don't know. You could bring your mom here and just have her look around. There's not a slip-on in sight."

"That's it! I'll do a survey of the shoes everybody's wearing. It will show her that not one kid wears slip-ons anymore," said Blanca.

"Just like those surveys we did last year," said Irma. "Can I help?"

"Sure. Let's get started."

Student Guide - page 2 *(Answers on p. 44)*

Blanca and Irma did their survey. They studied the kinds of shoes the students in their class wore the first day of school. This is what they found:

Kind of Shoe	Number of Pairs of Shoes
High-top Sneakers	9
Low-top Sneakers	8
Lace Boots	4
Sandals	3
Slip-ons	0

1. **A.** Do you think Blanca's data will help her convince her mother that slip-ons are not fashionable?
   B. Would a graph help?
2. What is the most common kind of shoe in Blanca's class?
3. If you surveyed your class, how do you think the data would compare with Blanca's?
4. What kind of shoes are stylish in your school?

Variables are things that change or vary in an experiment or survey. Blanca and Irma's survey has two main variables: "Kind of Shoe" and "Number of Pairs of Shoes." The kinds of shoes vary from high-top sneakers to lace boots to sandals.

All the kinds of shoes listed in the first column of the data table are values of the variable Kind of Shoe. The number of pairs of shoes varied from 0 to 9 pairs. We can say that 0, 3, 4, 8, 9 are values of the variable "number of pairs of shoes." So, the possible outcomes for each variable are called **values.**

Student Guide - page 3 *(Answers on p. 44)*

Teaching the Lab

Part 1   Using Variables: Slip-ons and Sneakers

The *Eyelets* Lab Pages in the *Student Guide* open with a vignette. Slip-ons and Sneakers uses the context of fashion to review using surveys to gather data to solve a problem *(Questions 1–4).*

Variables and values are also reviewed in the Slip-ons and Sneakers section. Point out that a **variable** is something that changes or varies in an experiment, like Kind of Shoe and Number of Pairs of Shoes. The possible outcomes for each variable are called **values.** To help students make the distinction between variables and values, *Question 5* asks students to make a table listing variables they may study in a survey in the first column and possible values for each variable in the second column. Figure 1 shows a few possible entries in such a table.

Variables and Possible Values

Variables	Values
Kind of Shoe	High-top Sneakers, Lace Boots
Number of Pairs of Shoes	0, 3, 5
Shirt Color	White, Red, Plaid
Height	56 in, 57 in
Number of Pockets	0, 1, 2, 4
Length of Hair	Short, Medium, Long
Type of Pants	Jeans, Dress Pants, Shorts

Figure 1: *Variables and values table*

TIMS Tip

If many of your students are new to *Math Trailblazers*, you may decide to complete optional Lesson 2 with your class. If so, save the variables and values data table generated in *Question 5.*

Question 6 asks students to identify the numerical and categorical variables in the table. For example, in the Figure 1 table, Number of Pockets is a **numerical** variable since the values are numbers. Length of Hair and Type of Pants are **categorical** variables since the values are not numbers. Note that if the values for Length of Hair were given as 15 in or 1 cm, then Length of Hair would be considered a numerical variable.

Part 2 Reviewing the TIMS Laboratory Method: *Eyelets*

The lab *Eyelets* gives an overview of the TIMS Laboratory Method. This method has four phases:

- Draw
- Collect
- Graph
- Explore

Each phase is discussed in a section of the *Eyelets* Lab Pages in the *Student Guide.*

The lab begins with a question: *"How many eyelets are on students' shoes in your class?"* The key variables related to this question are the Number of Eyelets (E) on a pair of shoes and the Number of Pairs of Shoes (P). The lab attempts to discover the relationship between these two variables.

Discuss the exact meaning of "the number of eyelets on a pair of shoes" with your students. In writing the lab, we assume that an eyelet is one of the little holes meant for a shoelace. According to this definition, holes for buckles or hook-and-loop strips are not eyelets. We also assume that the number of eyelets is the total number on both shoes. You may choose to use other definitions. However, you must clearly define the terms at the outset, just as the rules of a game must be agreed on before the game begins. Note that using our definition, the number of eyelets is always a multiple of 4. This result is the subject of **Questions 12** and **13** in the Explore section of the lab.

The opening question itself—*"How many eyelets are on students' shoes in your class?"*—may also need to be clarified. What is meant is a whole series of questions:

- *How many students are wearing shoes with no eyelets?*
- *How many students are wearing shoes with one eyelet?*
- *How many students are wearing shoes with two eyelets? etc.*

Another way to interpret the question is as a query about individual students: *"How many eyelets are on*

5. What else could you study about the way people look and the way they dress? Make a list of variables you could study. List two or three values for each variable. Make a table like the one shown.

Variables and Possible Values

Variables	Values
Kind of Shoe	High-top Sneakers, Lace Boots, Slip-ons
Number of Pairs of Shoes	0, 3, 5
Shirt Color	White, Red, Plaid
Height	56 inches, 58 inches

Numerical variables are variables with values that are numbers. Number of pairs of shoes and height are numerical variables. **Categorical variables** have values that are not numbers. Kind of shoe and shirt color are examples of categorical variables.

6. On the data table you made for Question 5, write an *N* beside the numerical variables. Write a *C* beside the categorical variables.

Eyelets

In this lab, you will answer a certain question about how the students in your class dress for school. As you do the lab, you will learn a method that you can use to find answers to other questions—questions about how people dress or questions that have nothing to do with clothing. We call this method the TIMS Laboratory Method. This method is very much like the method scientists use in their investigations.

Usually, an investigation begins with a question. For this investigation, we ask the question: *How many eyelets are on students' shoes in your class?*

To answer this question scientifically, we need to identify the important variables. The two main variables in the lab are:

- the total number of eyelets on a pair of shoes (E).
- the number of pairs of shoes (P).

Your class will conduct a survey to answer the question.

4   SG · Grade 5 · Unit 1 · Lesson 1   Eyelets

Student Guide - page 4 (Answers on p. 45)

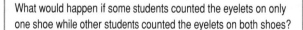

TIMS Tip

Students who used *Math Trailblazers* in fourth grade should be familiar with the concepts in the *Eyelets* lab. Students who are new to *Math Trailblazers* will need much more guidance. The TIMS Tutor: *The TIMS Laboratory Method* in the *Teacher Implementation Guide* includes a detailed description of the TIMS Laboratory Method and a discussion of the importance of variables.

Journal Prompt

What would happen if some students counted the eyelets on only one shoe while other students counted the eyelets on both shoes?

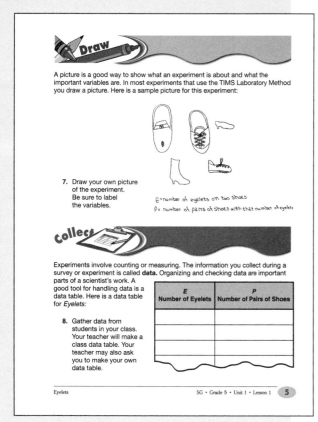

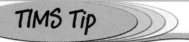

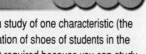

Student Guide - page 5 *(Answers on p. 45)*

TIMS Tip

During the activity, you may wish to ask the groups how well they are working together. It may be helpful to concentrate the discussion on one of the following questions: *"Did your group take turns? Did your group stay on task? Did everyone participate?"* If any group answers, "No," then encourage the group to make a plan to take turns, stay on task, or to include everyone.

Content Note

Shoe Populations. This lab is a study of one characteristic (the number of eyelets) of the population of shoes of students in the class. In this lab, sampling is not required because you can study the entire population. If, however, the population of interest is all the shoes in the school, then the shoes in the class are a sample. In the upcoming *Adventure Book* and lab, entire populations cannot be studied, so sampling is required.

Richard's shoes?" "How many are on Rachel's shoes?" and so on for all the students in the class. Although this information could be listed in a "raw data" table, our analysis does not focus on what any particular student is wearing. For this reason, we organize our data table and graph so we can study patterns in the number of eyelets of the whole group.

Draw. The work of beginning the investigation is summarized and communicated by a picture that shows the main variables and indicates the procedure *(Question 7).* See the *Student Guide* for a sample picture.

Collect. Before you begin gathering the data, set up a two-column data table like the one in Figure 2 and ask what numbers you should write in the Number of Eyelets column. Help students to see that odd numbers of eyelets are not possible and that zero eyelets is possible. The left-hand column can then be filled with 0, 2, 4, etc. As part of the analysis of the lab, students will find that listing the multiples of 4 would have been enough (since there is an even number of eyelets on each of two shoes).

Eyelets

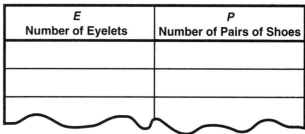

E Number of Eyelets	P Number of Pairs of Shoes

Figure 2: *Blank data table*

Once the data table is set up and students have counted all the eyelets on both their shoes, then gather the data by asking for a show of hands for each value of the variable Number of Eyelets in the data table ($E = 0$, $E = 2$, $E = 4$, etc.). When you exceed the maximum number of eyelets in the class—which may be 40 or more—then, ask:

How can you be sure each student was counted once and only once? (The sum of the numbers in the Number of Pairs of Shoes column should equal the number of students in the class.)

Once the class data table is complete, you may have students copy it *(Question 8).* Figure 3 shows sample data for a fifth-grade class.

Eyelets

E Number of Eyelets	*P* Number of Pairs of Shoes
0	1
2	0
4	0
6	0
8	1
10	0
12	0
14	0
16	3
18	0
20	3
22	0
24	4
26	0
28	7
30	0
32	6
34	0
36	3
38	0
40	0

Figure 3: *Sample data*

Graph. It does not make sense to think about "in between" values for the number of eyelets (e.g., 2.5 eyelets). Therefore a bar graph is appropriate for this data. Each student should graph the data on graph paper. If students have not used *Math Trailblazers* before, model the graphing for them, using a poster-size piece of graph paper or a transparency of *Centimeter Grid Paper.* Be sure students:

- Label the lines, not the spaces, when they scale both the horizontal and vertical axes;
- Draw their bars centered on the lines, as shown in Figure 4;

Scientists look for patterns in data. Graphing your data can help you see patterns that are hard to notice in the data table. The third step in the TIMS Laboratory Method is graphing.

9. Make a bar graph of your class data. Graph the Number of Eyelets (*E*) on the horizontal axis (←—→). Graph the Number of Pairs of Shoes (*P*) on the vertical axis (↕) .

The last step in the TIMS Laboratory Method is analyzing the whole experiment. This means understanding what happened and using your understanding to make predictions. Questions for new investigations may also come up during this step. Most labs have questions to help you better understand the important ideas. Your teacher may ask you to answer these questions alone or in small groups. Be ready to explain how you found your answers.

Use the class graph and data table to answer the following questions.

10. **A.** How many pairs of shoes have 20 eyelets?
 B. How many pairs of shoes have 8 eyelets?
 C. How many pairs of shoes have 0 eyelets?

11. **A.** What number of eyelets is most common in your class? (This number is called the **mode.**)
 B. How can you find the mode by looking at your graph?

12. **A.** List all the values for Number of Eyelets that have bars above them.
 B. What do you notice about these numbers? Explain.

13. Alexis told her class that she had 14 eyelets on her pair of shoes. Do you think she is correct? Why or why not?

Student Guide - page 6 (Answers on p. 46)

- Label each axis correctly; and
- Give the graph a title.

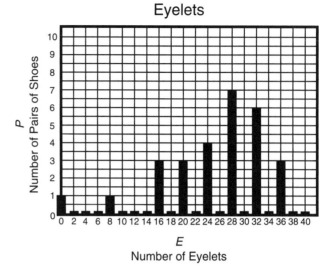

Figure 4: *A graph of the sample data in Figure 3*

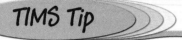
Explore. The analysis of the lab is structured by *Questions 10–19* in the Explore section of the *Student Guide.* As you discuss the questions, emphasize that the answers are often found in more than one way. Encouraging multiple solutions lets all students participate in ways they understand. Finding multiple solutions is facilitated by the multiple representations of the situation that were developed in the lab: the shoes themselves, the data table, and the graph. On the other hand, solutions found by different methods should agree. If a graph shows that ten people have shoes with 24 eyelets and a data table shows only 9 such people, then something is wrong.

To answer *Questions 10A–10C,* students can read the information directly from the data table or graph. For example, on the graph in Figure 4, the height of the bar above $E = 20$ eyelets shows us that 3 pairs of shoes have 20 eyelets. Similarly, 1 pair of shoes has 8 eyelets and 1 pair of shoes has 0 eyelets.

Question 11 introduces the term mode, a kind of average. The **mode** of a set of data is the most common value. In the sample data, the most common number of eyelets is 28. Seven pairs of shoes have 28 eyelets. This is the largest number of pairs of shoes in the data table. We can easily find the mode on the graph by identifying the tallest bar.

In *Question 12* students look for a pattern in the values of the variable Number of Eyelets. First, they list all the values for Number of Eyelets that have bars above them. In the sample data, these values are 0, 8, 16, 20, 24, 28, 32, and 36. Students might notice that these numbers are all multiples of four, although they may describe these values as divisible by four or the "numbers you get when you skip count by four." The multiples of four appear because there are an even number of eyelets on each of two shoes. If a student has reported a value for number of eyelets that is not a multiple of four, ask him or her to recount the eyelets. Students apply this result in **Question 13.** Since 14 is not a multiple of four, Alexis cannot have 14 eyelets on her shoes.

Question 14 asks students to describe the shape of the graph. This question will reoccur in many labs and activities throughout the year. The shape of the graph tells the "story of the data." At first, students' responses may be hesitant and incomplete, but as they practice in each successive lab, their responses will become more sophisticated. Parts A, B, and C of this question help students get started. To describe the graph in Figure 4, they can say that there are 8 bars on the graph that are not all the same height. The tallest bars are to the right on the graph (for larger numbers of eyelets) and the smallest bars are to the left (for smaller numbers of eyelets).

Questions 15–16 ask students to predict the shape of an Eyelets graph for different populations. For example, professional basketball players wear athletic shoes **(Question 15).** Since most players will wear the same kind of shoe, there probably will be fewer bars on the graph. Since the shoes will have lots of eyelets, the bars to the right on the graph will be tall. There will not be any bars on the left of the graph.

There are many strategies for finding the total number of eyelets on all the shoes of all the students in the class **(Question 17).** One possible strategy is to use a calculator to first multiply each number of eyelets by the corresponding number of pairs of shoes (the height of the bar for that number of eyelets). Then, sum the products as shown here for the sample data: $0 \times 1 + 8 \times 1 + 16 \times 3 + 20 \times 3 + 24 \times 4 + 28 \times 7 + 32 \times 6 + 36 \times 3 = 708$ eyelets. Although strategies may vary, there is only one correct solution. However, reasonable estimates and strategies may vary for **Question 18.** Students are to estimate the number of eyelets on all the shoes on all the fifth graders in the school. One solution for a school with four fifth-grade classrooms might indicate that since there are about 700 eyelets in one classroom, the number of eyelets in the fifth grade is about 4×700 or 2800 eyelets. Encourage students to share their solutions and strategies with one another.

14. Describe the shape of your graph.
    A. How many bars are on your graph?
    B. Are the bars all about the same height or are some bars much taller than others?
    C. Are the tallest bars at the beginning, middle, or end of the graph?

15. Describe the *Eyelets* graph for a professional basketball team. (Would the tallest bars be at the beginning, middle, or end of the graph? Would there be many bars or just one or two?)

16. Describe the *Eyelets* graph for data collected at the beach. (Would the tallest bars be at the beginning, middle, or end of the graph? Would there be many bars or just one or two?)

17. What is the total number of eyelets in your class?

18. Estimate how many eyelets are on all the shoes of all the fifth-grade students in your school. Explain how you made your estimate.

19. How would the graph be different if you gathered data from all the fifth graders in your school?

The TIMS Laboratory Method
You will use the TIMS Laboratory Method many times this year. In this lab, you used the TIMS Laboratory Method to study the number of eyelets on the shoes of the students in your class. There were four steps:

- **Draw.** The investigation started with a question. The question was made clearer by identifying variables that could be counted or measured. A picture showed what the experiment was about.
- **Collect.** You used data tables to organize the data.
- **Graph.** A graph showed patterns in the data more clearly than the table.
- **Explore.** You answered questions about the lab and thought about what might make things turn out differently.

Eyelets   SG • Grade 5 • Unit 1 • Lesson 1   **7**

Student Guide - page 7 (Answers on p. 46)

Journal Prompt

Write about what you did in this lab. Describe what you learned.

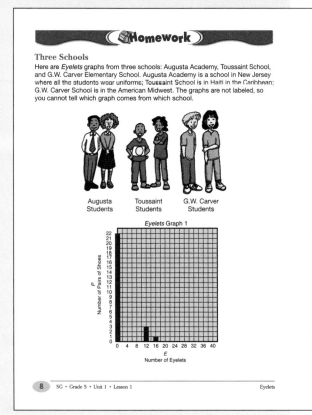

Student Guide - page 8 (Answers on p. 47)

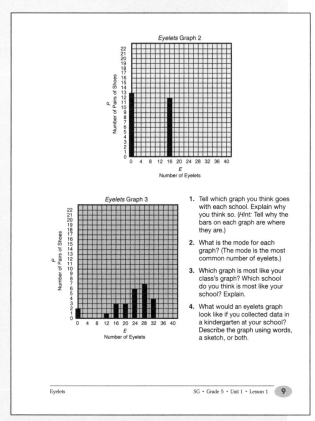

Student Guide - page 9 (Answers on p. 47)

Math Facts

Students using *Math Trailblazers* are expected to demonstrate fluency with all the math facts by the end of fourth grade. Beginning in Unit 2, the fifth grade materials provide a systematic review and assessment of the multiplication and division facts.

In Unit 1, Daily Practice and Problems items C and E provide an opportunity to identify any students who do not yet have fluency with the addition facts. For those students who do need extra practice with these facts, use the *Addition and Subtraction Math Facts Review* section in the *Facts Resource Guide* for fifth grade. This section includes diagnostic tests, activities, and games to identify and practice the facts they need to learn. Students should work on these facts using the suggested sequence of activities at home with their families or in school with resource teachers or parent volunteers. At the same time they should continue with the normal fifth-grade lessons using strategies, calculators, and printed fact tables to assist them as they solve problems. In this way they will not be prevented from learning more rigorous mathematics while working on the math facts.

Homework and Practice

- The Homework section in the *Student Guide* has several problems that ask students to interpret *Eyelets* graphs from three schools with differing populations.

- Daily Practice and Problems item F provides practice identifying numerical and categorical variables.

- Assign Parts 1 and 2 of the Home Practice. Part 1 provides mental math practice. Part 2 examines variables and values.

Answers for Parts 1 and 2 of the Home Practice are in the Answer Key at the end of this lesson and at the end of this unit.

Assessment

Use the *Pockets at St. Crispin's* Assessment Page at the end of the Lesson Guide in the *Unit Resource Guide* to assess individual students' abilities to draw bar graphs and analyze data.

Extension

Assign Task B and Challenge D from the Daily Practice and Problems. These items make good "Problems of the Day" or "Problems of the Week." Ask students to work on them throughout the day or during the week as homework. Encourage students to describe their problem-solving process.

Name _____ Date _____

Unit 1 Home Practice

PART 1 Addition and Subtraction
Solve the following problems in your head.

A. 30 + 90 = _____   B. 50 + 60 = _____   C. 160 − 90 = _____

D. 148 − 50 = _____   E. 240 + 80 = _____   F. 100 − 32 = _____

G. 650 + 250 = _____   H. 732 + 632 = _____   I. 389 + 11 = _____

On another sheet of paper, explain how you solved two of the problems in your head.

PART 2 Variables and Values in Your Home

1. A. David asks each of his family members what his or her favorite vegetable is. Is he collecting data on a numerical or categorical variable?

   B. List four possible values for this variable.

2. A. Alexis asks her classmates how long it takes them to get to school. What variable is she studying? Is it numerical or categorical?

   B. List four possible values for this variable. (*Hint:* How long does it take you to get to school? How long does it take your friends?)

3. A. Brandon asks his friends what type of sandwiches they are going to order at the fast-food restaurant. Is he collecting data on a numerical or categorical variable?

   B. List four possible values for this variable.

POPULATIONS AND SAMPLES   DAB • Grade 5 • Unit 1   **3**

Discovery Assignment Book - **page 3** *(Answers on p. 48)*

TIMS Tip

Read the *Daily Practice and Problems and Home Practice Guide* in the *Teacher Implementation Guide* for information and suggestions on using these components of the curriculum.

At a Glance

Math Facts and Daily Practice and Problems

1. Use Bit A from the Daily Practice and Problems for practice with mental math strategies.
2. Assign Task B and Challenge D to develop problem-solving and estimation skills.
3. Use Bits C and E to assess students' fluency with addition facts.
4. Assign Task F for practice with numerical and categorical variables.

Part 1. Using Variables: Slip-ons and Sneakers

1. Read and discuss the opening vignette on the *Eyelets* Activity Pages in the *Student Guide.* *(Questions 1–4)*
2. List variables your class might study. List possible values for each. *(Question 5)*
3. Distinguish between numerical and categorical variables. *(Question 6)*

Part 2. Reviewing the TIMS Laboratory Method: *Eyelets*

1. Discuss and clarify the initial question on the *Eyelets* Activity Pages in the *Student Guide:* "How many eyelets are on the shoes of the students in your class?"
2. Students draw a picture of the lab. *(Question 7)*
3. Gather the data by a show of hands and organize it in a class data table. Students can copy the class data table. *(Question 8)*
4. Students graph the data in a bar graph. *(Question 9)* You may need to model correct graphing techniques using a transparency of *Centimeter Grid Paper.*
5. Students answer *Questions 10–19* in the *Student Guide.* Discuss their answers, stressing that many problems can be solved in more than one way.

Homework

1. Assign *Questions 1–4* in the Homework section in the *Student Guide.*
2. Assign Parts 1 and 2 of the Home Practice in the *Discovery Assignment Book.*

Assessment

Use the *Pockets at St. Crispin's* Assessment Page found at the end of the Lesson Guide.

Extension

Assign Task B and Challenge D as "Problems of the Day" or "Problems of the Week."

Answer Key is on pages 44–49.

Notes:

Pockets at St. Crispin's

One day, the students in Mrs. Judd's fifth-grade class at St. Crispin School counted the pockets on their clothes. This is their data:

N Number of Pockets	S Number of Students
0	0
1	5
2	6
3	0
4	0
5	12
6	0
7	0

To understand this data, you must know that the students at St. Crispin's wear uniforms. The girls wear white blouses and plaid skirts; the boys wear dark blue pants and light blue shirts.

1. Make a bar graph of the data on a piece of graph paper.

2. How many students are in Mrs. Judd's class? _____

3. What is the most common number of pockets? _____

4. Describe the shape of the graph.

5. Why do you think the bars on the graph are where they are?

Centimeter Grid Paper

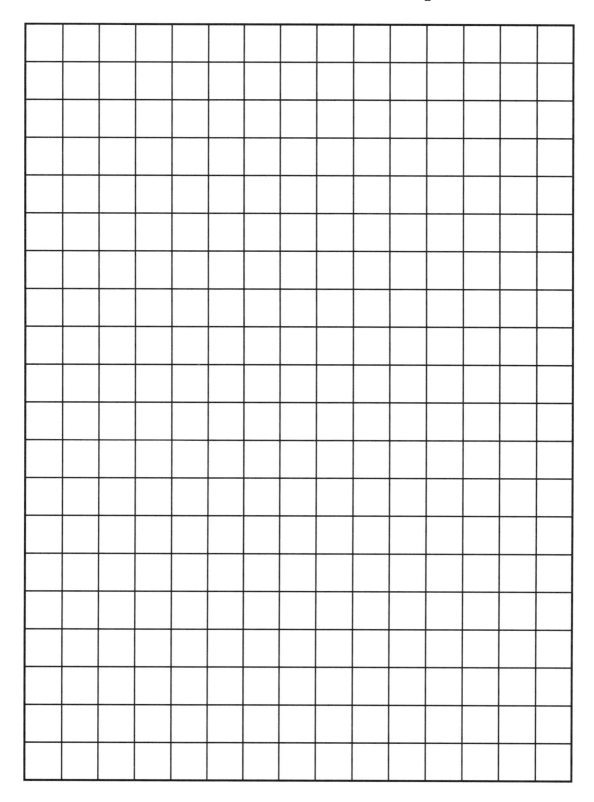

_____

Eyelets

Slip-ons and Sneakers

"I'm not sure those sneakers go with that outfit, Blanca," Mrs. Campos said. "Why don't you wear your slip-ons? I think that would look pretty."

"I hate those slip-ons, Mama," answered Blanca. "Nobody wears shoes like that anymore. Don't you want me to look stylish for my first day of fifth grade?"

"Of course I want you to look nice," Mrs. Campos answered. "That's no problem—you're a beautiful girl. But those sneakers . . ."

"Trust me, Mom," interrupted Blanca. "This look is cool."

Later, at school, Blanca met her friend Irma. "¡Hola! Irma. Guess what? My mom wanted me to wear slip-ons for the first day of school. She said sneakers don't go with my outfit."

"Oh, no!" said Irma. "How'd you convince her to let you wear them?"

"I told her to trust me, and she did—for today," said Blanca. "But I'm afraid she'll make me wear those ugly shoes sooner or later. How can I convince her that nobody wears slip-ons anymore?"

"I don't know. You could bring your mom here and just have her look around. There's not a slip-on in sight."

"That's it! I'll do a survey of the shoes everybody's wearing. It will show her that not one kid wears slip-ons anymore," said Blanca.

"Just like those surveys we did last year," said Irma. "Can I help?"

"Sure. Let's get started."

Student Guide - page 2

Blanca and Irma did their survey. They studied the kinds of shoes the students in their class wore the first day of school. This is what they found:

Kind of Shoe	Number of Pairs of Shoes
High-top Sneakers	9
Low-top Sneakers	8
Lace Boots	4
Sandals	3
Slip-ons	0

1. **A.** Do you think Blanca's data will help her convince her mother that slip-ons are not fashionable?
   B. Would a graph help?

2. What is the most common kind of shoe in Blanca's class?

3. If you surveyed your class, how do you think the data would compare with Blanca's?

4. What kind of shoes are stylish in your school?

Variables are things that change or vary in an experiment or survey. Blanca and Irma's survey has two main variables: "Kind of Shoe" and "Number of Pairs of Shoes." The kinds of shoes vary from high-top sneakers to lace boots to sandals.

All the kinds of shoes listed in the first column of the data table are values of the variable Kind of Shoe. The number of pairs of shoes varied from 0 to 9 pairs. We can say that 0, 3, 4, 8, 9 are values of the variable "number of pairs of shoes." So, the possible outcomes for each variable are called **values.**

Student Guide - page 3

Student Guide (pp. 2–3)

Eyelets

1. **A.** Yes

   B. Answers will vary. However, a graph would display her data in another way.

2. high-top sneakers

3. Answers will vary.

4. Answers will vary.

Student Guide (pp. 4–5)

5.* Answers will vary. Some possible solutions include:

Variable	Values
Color of Hair	blond, brown, black, gray, red
Color of Eyes	blue, green, brown
Number of Buttons on Clothes	0, 1, 2, 3

6.* Answers will vary. For possible solutions listed above,

Variable	Values	
Color of Hair	blond, brown, black, gray, red	C
Color of Eyes	blue, green, brown	C
Number of Buttons on Clothes	0, 1, 2, 3	N

7. Students' pictures will vary. See the *Student Guide* for a sample picture.*

8. See Figure 3 in Lesson Guide 1 for a sample data table.*

---

5. What else could you study about the way people look and the way they dress? Make a list of variables you could study. List two or three values for each variable. Make a table like the one shown.

Variables and Possible Values

Variables	Values
Kind of Shoe	High-top Sneakers, Lace Boots, Slip-ons
Number of Pairs of Shoes	0, 3, 5
Shirt Color	White, Red, Plaid
Height	56 inches, 58 inches

Numerical variables are variables with values that are numbers. Number of pairs of shoes and height are numerical variables. **Categorical variables** have values that are not numbers. Kind of shoe and shirt color are examples of categorical variables.

6. On the data table you made for Question 5, write an *N* beside the numerical variables. Write a *C* beside the categorical variables.

Eyelets

In this lab, you will answer a certain question about how the students in your class dress for school. As you do the lab, you will learn a method that you can use to find answers to other questions—questions about how people dress or questions that have nothing to do with clothing. We call this method the TIMS Laboratory Method. This method is very much like the method scientists use in their investigations.

Usually, an investigation begins with a question. For this investigation, we ask the question: *How many eyelets are on students' shoes in your class?*

To answer this question scientifically, we need to identify the important variables. The two main variables in the lab are:

- the total number of eyelets on a pair of shoes (*E*)
- the number of pairs of shoes (*P*).

Your class will conduct a survey to answer the question.

Student Guide - page 4

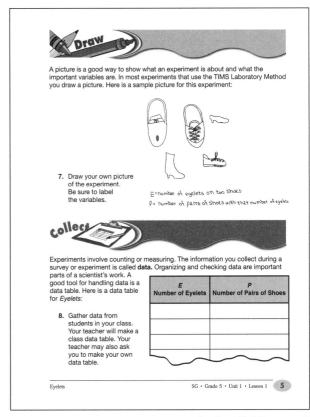

A picture is a good way to show what an experiment is about and what the important variables are. In most experiments that use the TIMS Laboratory Method you draw a picture. Here is a sample picture for this experiment:

7. Draw your own picture of the experiment. Be sure to label the variables.

E= number of eyelets on two shoes
P= number of pairs of shoes with that number of eyelets

Experiments involve counting or measuring. The information you collect during a survey or experiment is called **data.** Organizing and checking data are important parts of a scientist's work. A good tool for handling data is a data table. Here is a data table for *Eyelets:*

E Number of Eyelets	P Number of Pairs of Shoes

8. Gather data from students in your class. Your teacher will make a class data table. Your teacher may also ask you to make your own data table.

Student Guide - page 5

*Answers and/or discussion are included in the Lesson Guide.

Scientists look for patterns in data. Graphing your data can help you see patterns that are hard to notice in the data table. The third step in the TIMS Laboratory Method is graphing.

9. Make a bar graph of your class data. Graph the Number of Eyelets (*E*) on the horizontal axis (⟷). Graph the Number of Pairs of Shoes (*P*) on the vertical axis (↕) .

The last step in the TIMS Laboratory Method is analyzing the whole experiment. This means understanding what happened and using your understanding to make predictions. Questions for new investigations may also come up during this step. Most labs have questions to help you better understand the important ideas. Your teacher may ask you to answer these questions alone or in small groups. Be ready to explain how you found your answers.

Use the class graph and data table to answer the following questions.

10. **A.** How many pairs of shoes have 20 eyelets?
    B. How many pairs of shoes have 8 eyelets?
    C. How many pairs of shoes have 0 eyelets?

11. **A.** What number of eyelets is most common in your class? (This number is called the **mode.**)
    B. How can you find the mode by looking at your graph?

12. **A.** List all the values for Number of Eyelets that have bars above them.
    B. What do you notice about these numbers? Explain.

13. Alexis told her class that she had 14 eyelets on her pair of shoes. Do you think she is correct? Why or why not?

6   SG • Grade 5 • Unit 1 • Lesson 1   Eyelets

Student Guide - page 6

14. Describe the shape of your graph.
    A. How many bars are on your graph?
    B. Are the bars all about the same height or are some bars much taller than others?
    C. Are the tallest bars at the beginning, middle, or end of the graph?

15. Describe the *Eyelets* graph for a professional basketball team. (Would the tallest bars be at the beginning, middle, or end of the graph? Would there be many bars or just one or two?)

16. Describe the *Eyelets* graph for data collected at the beach. (Would the tallest bars be at the beginning, middle, or end of the graph? Would there be many bars or just one or two?)

17. What is the total number of eyelets in your class?

18. Estimate how many eyelets are on all the shoes of all the fifth-grade students in your school. Explain how you made your estimate.

19. How would the graph be different if you gathered data from all the fifth graders in your school?

The TIMS Laboratory Method
You will use the TIMS Laboratory Method many times this year. In this lab, you used the TIMS Laboratory Method to study the number of eyelets on the shoes of the students in your class. There were four steps:

• **Draw.** The investigation started with a question. The question was made clearer by identifying variables that could be counted or measured. A picture showed what the experiment was about.
• **Collect.** You used data tables to organize the data.
• **Graph.** A graph showed patterns in the data more clearly than the table.
• **Explore.** You answered questions about the lab and thought about what might make things turn out differently.

Eyelets   SG • Grade 5 • Unit 1 • Lesson 1   7

Student Guide - page 7

*Answers and/or discussion are included in the Lesson Guide.

Student Guide (pp. 6–7)

9. See Figure 4 in Lesson 1 for a sample graph.*

The answers to *Questions 10–14* and *17–19* are based on the sample data in Figures 3 and 4 in Lesson Guide 1.

10.* **A.** Answers will vary. Using sample data, 3 pairs of shoes.

   B. Answers will vary. Using sample data, 1 pair of shoes.

   C. Answers will vary. Using sample data, 1 pair of shoes.

11.* **A.** Answers will vary. Using sample data, 28 eyelets.

   B. The Number of Eyelets with the tallest bar is the mode.

12.* **A.** Answers will vary. Using sample data: 0, 8, 16, 20, 24, 28, 32, 36.

   B. Answers will vary. Possible responses include: They are all even. They are all multiples of four.

13. No. Although 14 is even, it is not a multiple of four.*

14.* **A.** Answers will vary. Using sample data, 8 bars.

   B. Answers will vary. Using sample data, some bars are taller than others.

   C. Answers will vary. Using sample data, the tallest bars are at the right on the graph.

15. Answers will vary. Possible responses include: The tallest bars would be at the end of the graph since most professional basketball players wear big shoes. There would probably be a few bars since different brands of sneakers probably have different numbers of eyelets.*

16. Answers will vary. Possible responses include: The tallest bars would be at the beginning because sandals usually don't have eyelets. There would be a few bars since some people would wear shoes with eyelets.

17. Answers will vary. Using sample data, 708 eyelets.*

18. Answers will vary. One possible response is: If one class has 708 eyelets and there are 4 fifth-grade classrooms in the school, then there are about 2800 eyelets.*

19. Answers will vary. One possible response is: The shape of the graph would be the same as a graph for fifth-graders' shoes, but all the bars would be taller.

Student Guide (pp. 8–9)

Homework

1. Graph 1 goes with Toussaint School because many of the students wear sandals with no eyelets. The bar for zero is the tallest bar. Graph 2 goes with Augusta Academy because the students wear uniforms and the same shoes. So, there is one bar for boys with 16 eyelets and one for girls with no eyelets. (See the illustration in the *Student Guide.*) Graph 3 goes with G.W. Carver School because students wear a variety of shoes. The bars are all over the graph showing the variety of shoes.

2. Graph 1: The mode is 0 eyelets. Graph 2: The mode is 0 eyelets. Graph 3: The mode is 28 eyelets.

3. Answers will vary. Graph 3 is most like the sample graph in Figure 4 of Lesson Guide 1 because the bars are spread across the graph with the highest bars on the right side.

4. Answers will vary. One possible solution is that the graph would have many bars since students wear all kinds of shoes. Since the shoes are smaller than the shoes of fifth graders, the number of eyelets would be smaller and the bars would be to the left of the bars on a graph for the fifth-graders' shoes.

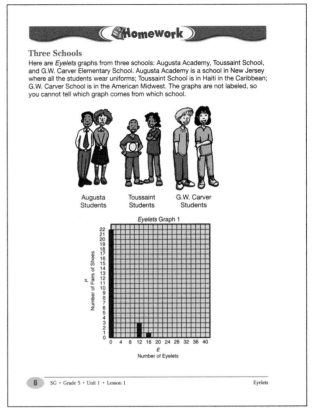

Student Guide - page 8

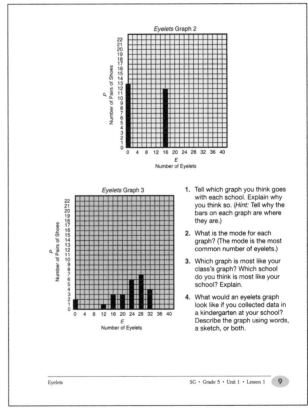

Student Guide - page 9

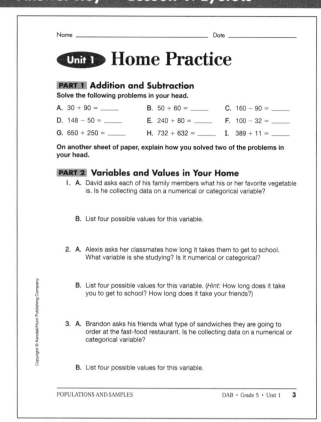

Discovery Assignment Book - page 3

Discovery Assignment Book (p. 3)

Home Practice*

Part 1. Addition and Subtraction

A.	120	**B.**	110
C.	70	**D.**	98
E.	320	**F.**	68
G.	900	**H.**	1364
I.	400		

Part 2. Variables and Values in Your Home

1. **A.** Type of vegetable; categorical.

   B. Answers will vary. Four possible responses include: carrots, broccoli, celery, and cauliflower.

2. **A.** Time in minutes; numerical.

   B. Answers will vary. Four possible responses include: 15 minutes, 20 minutes, 1 hour, and 5 minutes.

3. **A.** Type of sandwich; categorical.

   B. Answers will vary. Four possible responses include: ham, turkey, tuna, and cheese.

*Answers for all the Home Practice in the *Discovery Assignment Book* are at the end of the unit.

Unit Resource Guide (p. 41)

Pockets at St. Crispin's

1.

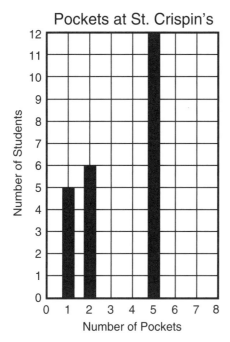

Pockets at St. Crispin's

2. 23 students

3. 5 pockets

4. Descriptions will vary. There are 3 bars on the graph. Each bar is a different height. The tallest bar is for 5 pockets.

5. Answers will vary. One possible description is: Since students wear uniforms, then the number of pockets depends on the style of uniform each student wears. For example, five pockets may be a boy wearing pants and a dress shirt. The pants could have two side pockets and one rear pocket. The shirt could have two front pockets. A girl could wear a skirt with no pockets and a shirt with one or two pockets.

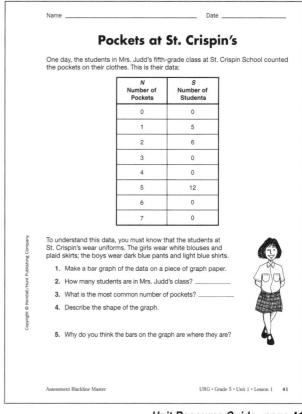

Pockets at St. Crispin's

Name _____ Date _____

One day, the students in Mrs. Judd's fifth-grade class at St. Crispin School counted the pockets on their clothes. This is their data:

N Number of Pockets	S Number of Students
0	0
1	5
2	6
3	0
4	0
5	12
6	0
7	0

To understand this data, you must know that the students at St. Crispin's wear uniforms. The girls wear white blouses and plaid skirts; the boys wear dark blue pants and light blue shirts.

1. Make a bar graph of the data on a piece of graph paper.
2. How many students are in Mrs. Judd's class? _____
3. What is the most common number of pockets? _____
4. Describe the shape of the graph.

5. Why do you think the bars on the graph are where they are?

Assessment Blackline Master   URG • Grade 5 • Unit 1 • Lesson 1   41

Unit Resource Guide - page 41

Optional Lesson 2

Review: Representing Data

Lesson Overview

Estimated Class Sessions

2-3

This review lesson is for students who are new to the *Math Trailblazers* curriculum. In Part 1 students collect, organize, and graph numerical data. In Part 2 students investigate averages using data about their own classroom and data about a fictional classroom. They use the median to average data. (This review lesson is adapted from Lessons 2 and 3 of Unit 1 in the fourth-grade curriculum.)

Key Content

- Using numerical variables.
- Naming values of variables.
- Collecting, organizing, graphing, and analyzing data.
- Making and interpreting bar graphs.
- Investigating the concept of averages.
- Averaging: finding the median.

Key Vocabulary

- average
- median
- numerical variable
- value
- variable

Math Facts

Use the Addition and Subtraction Math Facts Review section of the *Facts Resource Guide* as needed.

Homework

Assign the Homework sections of the *Collecting, Organizing, and Graphing Data* Activity Pages and the *Finding the Median* Activity Pages.

Assessment

Use the *Observational Assessment Record* and students' *Individual Assessment Record Sheets* to record students' abilities to make bar graphs.

Curriculum Sequence

Before This Unit

Bar Graphs

Part 1, which focuses on graphing numerical data in bar graphs, is taken directly from a fourth-grade activity (Unit 1 Lesson 2). Your class should complete Part 1 of this lesson if your students are new to *Math Trailblazers*.

Averages

Students have used medians to average data collected in labs in Grades 1, 2, 3, and 4. (See Unit 10 Lesson 4 in Grade 4 for an example.) In Grade 4 they were formally introduced to both medians and means in three activities (Unit 1 Lesson 3 and Unit 5 Lessons 2 and 3). Part 2 of this activity is taken largely from the introductory activity on finding medians in Unit 1 Lesson 3 of fourth grade.

After This Unit

Averages

If your students used the *Math Trailblazers* curriculum in previous years, the brief review of finding the median in Lesson 3 of this unit may be sufficient. Your students should not have to complete Part 2 of this lesson, which is a repeat of a fourth-grade activity. The mean is reviewed in Unit 4 of fifth grade. Students will continue to use averages in labs and activities throughout the year. (See *Distance vs. Time* in Unit 3 and *Spreading Out* in Unit 4 for specific examples.)

Materials List

Supplies and Copies

Student	Teacher
Supplies for Each Student	**Supplies** • class-generated data table, Variables and Possible Values, from Lesson 1
Copies • 1 copy of *Collecting, Organizing, and Graphing Data* per student (*Unit Resource Guide* Pages 63–65) • 1 copy of *Finding the Median* per student (*Unit Resource Guide* Pages 66–69) • 2 copies of *Centimeter Graph Paper* per student (*Unit Resource Guide* Page 70)	**Copies/Transparencies** • 1 transparency of *Bar Graph I: What's Wrong Here?* (*Unit Resource Guide* Page 61) • 1 transparency of *Bar Graph II: What's Wrong Here?* (*Unit Resource Guide* Page 62) • 1 transparency of *Three-column Data Table* or laminated data table wall chart or poster-size paper (*Unit Resource Guide* Page 71) • several transparencies of *Two-column Data Table* or laminated data table wall chart or poster-size paper (*Unit Resource Guide* Page 43) • 1 transparency of *Centimeter Graph Paper* or laminated graph wall chart or poster-size paper (*Unit Resource Guide* Page 70) • 1 copy of *Observational Assessment Record* to be used throughout this unit (*Unit Resource Guide* Pages 13–14)

All blackline masters including assessment, transparency, and DPP masters are also on the Teacher Resource CD.

Assessment Tools

Observational Assessment Record (*Unit Resource Guide* Pages 13–14)

Individual Assessment Record Sheet (*Teacher Implementation Guide,* Assessment section)

You will need the list of **variables** and **values** your class generated in Lesson 1 to complete Part 1 of this lesson.

Part 1 Collecting, Organizing, and Graphing Data

Choosing a Variable to Study. Distribute copies of the *Collecting, Organizing, and Graphing Data* Activity Pages that are at the end of the Lesson Guide. *Question 1* asks students to choose a **numerical variable** they would like to study. Refer to the data table Variables and Possible Values generated in Lesson 1 (*Question 5* on the *Eyelets* Activity Pages in the *Student Guide*). The variables listed describe the way people look and dress. Your class can choose a numerical variable from this list that is of particular interest or you can generate more numerical variables and add them to your table. Suggest students think of numerical variables to describe themselves or their families. Some common examples are number of family members, number of pets, height, and number of times moved. The values of these variables are numbers (e.g., the number of pets could be 0, 1, 2, 3, etc.).

Two sample data tables and a graph are provided on the *Collecting, Organizing, and Graphing Data* Activity Pages. These display Room 305's data on the number of blocks they live from school. You may wish to review and discuss Room 305's sample data before your class chooses a variable and collects data. However, some teachers choose to engage their students in the actual data collection before reviewing the activity pages. Then the sample data tables and graphs on the activity pages can be used to provide closure to the activity.

It is important to select a well-defined numerical variable. If you collect data on family size, you need to define this variable. A student's definition of family could include members outside the immediate family, especially if relatives such as a grandmother or an uncle reside in the student's home. You can eliminate any confusion by deciding upon a definition, such as the following: "As long as the person lives in a student's home full-time, he or she is considered part of the family." Number of pets is another variable that may need some definition. Does a student who has an aquarium count all the fish in his or her tank or do fish count as one pet?

TIMS Tip

It is important that the variable you choose involves quick and easy data collection. For instance, if you choose number of pencils in your desk as the numerical variable, you can easily ask each student to count his or her pencils and tell you the number. A numerical variable such as the number of pets in your house may be a good choice for your classroom to study. However, the number of pets may not vary much in some classrooms in some communities. (Many students might not have any pets or they may have only 1 or 2.) Choosing height, hand area, or the number of windows in students' homes would require more time, since students would need to gather data.

Collecting Data. Before collecting the raw data on the variable your class chooses, create a class data table on a wall chart or transparency. If you use transparencies of the *Two-column Data Table,* make sure you have enough copies to record data for every student. In the first column, list students' names. In the heading of the second column, list the name of the variable you are studying. Then in the second column, record each student's individual data beside his or her name. Room 305's data on the number of pets is shown in Figure 5.

Name	Number of Pets
Manny	2
Alexis	0
Lin	1
Frank	0

Figure 5: *Raw data for Room 305's pet data*

TIMS Tip

We chose to record the class raw data (see Figure 5). Then, we organized it in another data table using tallies to find the total number of students that corresponded to each value (see Figure 6). You may choose to simplify the data collection by eliminating the raw data table and using a two-column data table to collect data by a show of hands. Label the first column with the name of the variable. Fill in this column with the possible values of the variable. Label the second column, "Number of Students." Ask for a show of hands for each value and record the number of students for each, eliminating the need for tallies.

Next, your class needs to organize the data by creating a new table like that in Figure 6. Make a three-column data table using a wall chart or a transparency of a *Three-column Data Table.* Label the three headings as follows: the name of the variable you are studying (e.g., Number of Pets), Tally, and Number of Students. In the first column, list in numerical order all the values from your raw data table. Then using the raw data, tally the number of students that have the same value for the variable. (See Figure 6.) The total of the tally marks should equal the number of students in the class.

Number of Pets	Tally	Number of Students
0	// |	4
1	////	4
2	ЖЖ |	7
3	//	2
4	|	1
5	///	3
6	/	1

Figure 6: *Number of pets data table*

Graphing the Data. Use a transparency of *Centimeter Graph Paper* to get students started in setting up their bar graphs. Be sure to discuss the following before students create their own graphs: giving the graph a title, labeling and scaling axes, and drawing the bars. (See Figure 7 for a sample bar graph of the pets data.)

Review correct techniques for making bar graphs using the transparencies *Bar Graph I* and *II: What's Wrong Here?* These transparencies show incorrect bar graphs that display the data Room 305 collected on the number of blocks they live from school. Students may compare the correct bar graph "Number of Blocks We Live from School" on the *Collecting, Organizing, and Graphing Data* Activity Pages with the graphs on the transparencies.

In *Bar Graph I: What's Wrong Here?* the student listed each name and graphed a bar for each person's data. This does not organize the data any better than the raw data table. Also, the two variables we want to graph are not name and number of blocks but rather number of students and number of blocks. Consider these as mistakes in data analysis rather than in graphing.

Bar Graph II: What's Wrong Here? does not list the values in order on the horizontal axis, which makes the graph harder to read than the graph shown on the activity pages. Although we found out that no students live 6 blocks away from school, *Bar Graph II* does not show this. A small line, the width of a bar, can be placed on the horizontal axis above the 6 to denote that no students live 6 blocks away from school.

Students are now ready to graph the data they collected. While students graph the data, create a class graph of the data on a transparency of *Centimeter Graph Paper* or on poster-size graph paper. This class graph will serve as a reference for class discussion. Use *Questions 4–7* on the *Collecting, Organizing, and Graphing Data* Activity Pages to start a discussion about what you have learned about the class. *Questions 8–11* ask similar questions about Room 305's data on the number of blocks the students live from school.

Question 9 asks students if Room 305's graph would be as easy to read if the numbers (values) on the horizontal axis were not in numerical order. Students might recall that the *Bar Graph II: What's Wrong Here?* transparency gave an example of such a graph. It is much easier to read and interpret a graph when the values on the axes are in numerical order.

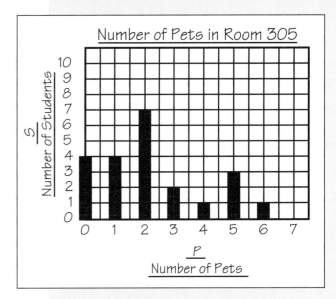

Figure 7: *Sample bar graph*

The shape of Room 305's graph tells us more when the numbers are in order. The graph tells us *(Question 10)* that the majority of the students in Room 305 live near school—3 blocks or closer. Not as many students live between 5 and 7 blocks away. Then, the final bar shows that several students live quite far. These students might get to school by bus.

Part 2 Finding the Median Value of a Set of Data

Refer to the class data tables and graph that were created in Part 1 of this lesson. As part of the data analysis of the survey, your class will find the median value of your class data.

To begin, ask students when and how they have heard the term average. This should generate a list of responses that may include batting average, average rainfall, grade point average, average student, average height, and so on. **Averages** indicate what is representative or typical in a given situation. Advise students that they will learn how to use one number to describe what is typical in a set of numbers. For example, when a student says that she averages about three goals per game, she doesn't mean that she scores three goals every game. She means that the typical number of goals she scores is three.

Review your class data table and graph from Part 1 along with the list of numerical variables your class generated. Choose two or three numerical variables that interest you and your students. Tell students they are going to find an average or typical value for each variable. Choose numerical variables with values that students can easily report and that have a relatively wide range of values. Height is a good variable for this activity since it is easy to recognize the median height of a group of students when they are standing in a line in order from shortest to tallest. If you use the variable your class graphed in Part 1 of this lesson, you will be able to find the median on your class graph as well as through the following procedure. In this discussion we will use the following variables as examples: height, number of pets, and number of pencils in your desk.

Ask students to write as large as possible the number of pets on one side of a piece of paper and the number of pencils in their desks on the other side. (Make sure students label the numbers so they know which is which.) Define the variables precisely. For example, the number of pencils in a desk should not include pens or markers.

Tell students that the median is one kind of average and they are going to find the median value for each variable. Define the **median** as the value exactly in the middle of the data. Ultimately you will find medians for the whole class, but first demonstrate the procedure using five students lined up in front of the room. Choose five students with varying heights and ask them to arrange themselves in order from shortest to tallest. The third student in line—the student in the middle—is the student with the median height. Note that in this example, we only have to measure the middle student to find the median height.

Next, find the median value for one of the other variables such as number of pets. Have the five students show the number of pets they own by holding up the data they wrote on pieces of paper. The students rearrange themselves in order with the student with the smallest number of pets at one end of the line and the student with the largest number of pets at the other end. The student in the middle of the line is holding the median number of pets. Note that more than one student may have the median number of pets. If the students in the line have 0, 1, 1, 2, and 2 pets, respectively, the median is 1 pet. Repeat the procedure to find the median number of pencils in students' desks.

Demonstrate how to find the median of an even number of values. Ask six students to show their data for the number of pencils in their desks. Here are three sample data sets and the corresponding medians.

Data Set A: 0, 1, 3, 5, 6, 10
The median is 4 pencils. Since there is not one middle data point, look at the numbers the two students in the middle of the line are holding (3 and 5). The median (4) is the number halfway between these two numbers.

Data Set B: 0, 1, 2, 2, 5, 6
The median is 2 pencils. Since the two middle data points are both 2, this is the median.

Data Set C: 0, 1, 3, 4, 6, 10
The median is $3\frac{1}{2}$ pencils since $3\frac{1}{2}$ is midway between the two middle data points (3 and 4).

Once students understand the process, ask them all to stand with their data. First, students find the median height by comparing heights with one another, arranging themselves in order from shortest to tallest, and identifying the student or students with the median height. Then students find the medians for the other two variables in a similar fashion using the numbers they wrote down.

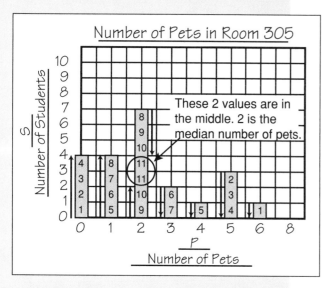

Figure 8: *The median number of pets is 2.*

Journal Prompt

What is an average?

Use the graphs your class made in Part 1 to find the medians and reinforce the concept that the median is the center of the data. The Number of Pets graph in Figure 8 illustrates how to find the median of a set of data using a graph. To find the middle value, count off each piece of data, one from the left and one from the right, until you reach the middle. Since the two middle values fall on the bar for 2 pets, 2 is the median number of pets for this class.

The concept of "average" is described on the *Finding the Median* Activity Pages. Use **Questions 1–5** to introduce procedures for finding the median and to explore the uses of averages in describing a set of data. To answer **Question 1A,** students must identify the child with the median height in an illustration of five students lined up in a row from shortest to tallest. Alexis has the median height because she is standing in the middle of the line. **Question 1B** asks students to reflect on the idea that the average height is the typical height for the group. If students do not agree with the idea that the middle height is the average or typical height, ask:

- *Which height would represent the heights of the group better? Why?*

- *If you can use just one height to represent the heights of the students in the group, which height would you choose?*

Students should come to realize from this discussion and later examples that using the middle height does make sense.

Question 5 asks students to use the data table or the graph to find the median number of blocks the students in Room 305 live from school. Students can either count off each tally mark, one at the top of the table and one at the bottom, until they reach the center or they can count the number of blocks represented by each bar in the graph. Figure 9 shows that the middle two values are both on the bar representing 3 blocks from school so the median number of blocks is 3. At this point, students can work in pairs to solve the remaining problems.

- After completing Part 1, students may complete *Questions 1–3* in the Homework section on the *Collecting, Organizing, and Graphing Data* Activity Pages. Each student will need one piece of *Centimeter Graph Paper* to complete the assignment.

- After completing Part 2 of this lesson, students may complete *Questions 1–2* on the *Finding the Median* Activity Pages.

Assessment

Use the *Observational Assessment Record* and students' *Individual Assessment Record Sheets* to record students' abilities to make bar graphs. The *Observational Assessment Record* follows the Unit Background for this unit and is on the Teacher Resource CD. For the *Individual Assessment Record Sheet,* see the Assessment section in the *Teacher Implementation Guide* or the Teacher Resource CD.

Extension

Collect data for other variables that may be used to describe the students in your class. Students can make bar graphs of both numerical and categorical data.

Room 305: Number of Blocks We Live from School

Number of Blocks	Tally	Number of Students
1					3
2	ℍ ||	7
3	⦶)||	4
4				2
5			1
6		0
7			1
8						4

The 2 circled tally marks are the 11th and 12th tallies.

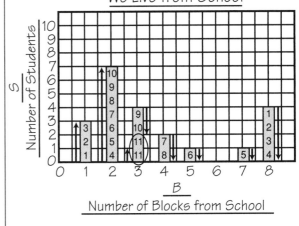

Room 305: Number of Blocks We Live from School

Figure 9: *Using a data table or graph to find the median. The median is 3 blocks.*

At a Glance

Part 1. Collecting, Organizing, and Graphing Data

1. Refer to the data table of variables and corresponding values that your class generated in *Question 5* of Lesson 1.

2. Working in groups, students think of numerical variables that describe themselves. Add these variables to the data table.

3. The class chooses a numerical variable to study. (*Question 1* on the *Collecting, Organizing, and Graphing Data* Activity Pages)

4. The class collects data. *(Question 2)* See Figures 5 and 6 for examples of a raw data table and one using tallies.

5. Use a transparency of *Centimeter Graph Paper* to get students started in setting up their graphs. Be sure to discuss the following before students create their own graphs: giving the graph a title, labeling and scaling axes, and drawing the bars.

6. Use the transparencies *Bar Graph I* and *II: What's Wrong Here?* in your discussion of bar graphs.

7. Students graph the class data. *(Question 3)* You may graph the class data as well.

8. Use *Questions 4–11* on the *Collecting, Organizing, and Graphing Data* Activity Pages to discuss what you have learned from the data about your class and Room 305.

Part 2. Finding the Median Value of a Set of Data

1. Discuss the term "average." Averages indicate what is representative or typical in a given situation.

2. Choose two or three numerical variables of interest to your students to use in examples as they learn to find averages.

3. Define the median as one type of average. It is the value exactly in the middle of the data.

4. Illustrate the procedure for finding the median by asking five students to line up in front of the class from shortest to tallest. The student in the middle of the line has the median height.

5. Use a similar procedure to find the medians of the data collected on the other variables you chose to study. Again use only five students in your example.

6. Demonstrate the procedure for finding the median of an even number of values using six students.

7. Ask all the students to stand with their data. Use the procedure described above to find the median values for height and the other two variables you chose.

8. Demonstrate how to find the median on a bar graph. Find the median value on the class graph you made in Part 1.

9. Read and discuss the information on the *Finding the Median* Activity Pages.

10. Use *Questions 1–5* to guide a class discussion on medians.

11. Students work in pairs to answer *Questions 6–7.*

Homework

Assign the Homework sections of the *Collecting, Organizing, and Graphing Data* Activity Pages and the *Finding the Median* Activity Pages.

Assessment

Use the *Observational Assessment Record* and students' *Individual Assessment Record Sheets* to record students' abilities to make bar graphs.

Extension

Have students collect and graph data for other variables that describe their class.

Answer Key is on pages 72–75.

Bar Graph I:
What's Wrong Here?

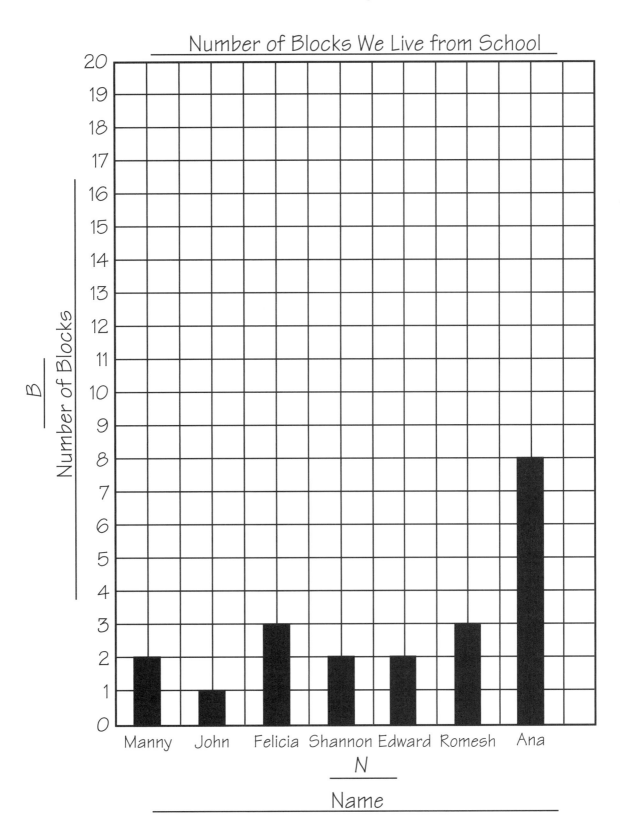

Number of Blocks We Live from School

Bar Graph II:
What's Wrong Here?

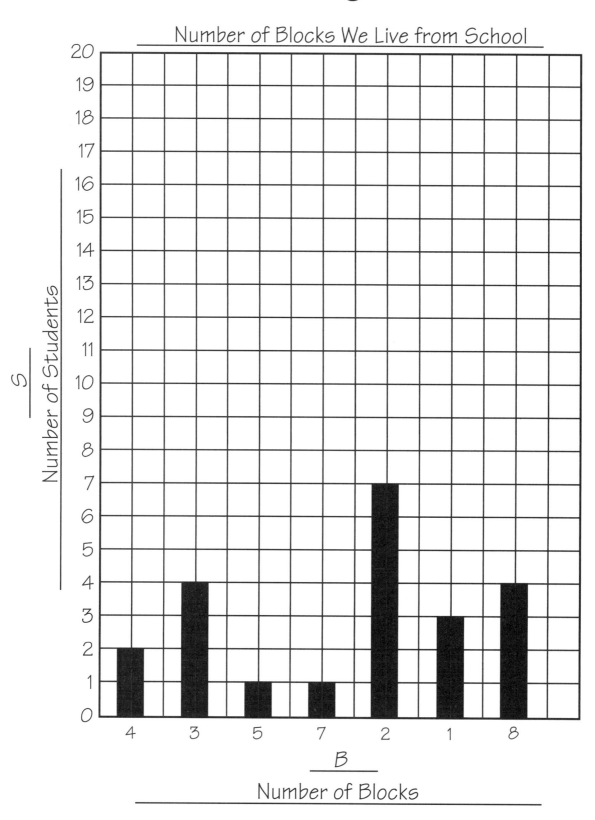

Transparency Master

Collecting, Organizing, and Graphing Data

Room 305's Data

Name	Number of Blocks
Manny	2
John	1
Felicia	3
Shannon	2
Edward	2
Romesh	3
Ana	8
Jackie	1
Nicholas	2
Lin	8
Blanca	2
David	3
Jessie	7
Brandon	1
Nila	2
Michael	8
Roberto	3
Irma	2
Arti	4
Lee Yah	4
Frank	5
Alexis	8

Mr. Moreno's class (Room 305) wanted to know how far the students in their class lived from school. They chose to study the variable number of blocks from school. First they recorded and organized their data in data tables.

Number of Blocks We Live from School

Number of Blocks B	Tally	Number of Students S
1	///	3
2	//// //	7
3	////	4
4	//	2
5	/	1
6		0
7	/	1
8	////	4

Then Mr. Moreno's class graphed the data in a bar graph.

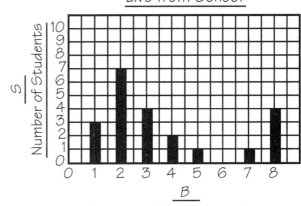

Number of Blocks We Live from School

1. With your class, choose a numerical variable to study.
   • Choose from the variables your class listed for Question 5 in Lesson 1.

   or

   • Make a new list of variables you would like to study about your classmates. Choose from this new list.

2. With your class, collect the data and organize it using data tables.

3. Graph the data in a bar graph. Be sure to title your graph and label the axes.

4. **A.** Which variable is on the horizontal axis on your graph? (⟷)

   B. Is this variable a categorical or a numerical variable? How do you know?

5. **A.** Which variable is on the vertical axis on your graph? (↕)

   B. Is this variable a categorical or a numerical variable? How do you know?

6. **A.** Which bar is the tallest on your graph?

   B. What does the tallest bar represent?

7. **A.** Which bar is the shortest on your graph?

   B. What does the shortest bar represent?

8. **A.** Look back at Room 305's graph called Number of Blocks We Live from School. Is the variable on the horizontal axis numerical or categorical? How can you tell?

   B. Is the variable on the vertical axis numerical or categorical? How can you tell?

9. Would Room 305's graph be as easy to read if the numbers (values) on the horizontal axis were not in order? Explain.

10. What does the graph tell you about the students in Room 305?

11. **A.** How many students in Room 305 live 3 blocks from school or less?

   B. Is this more or less than half the class? Explain your thinking.

You will need one sheet of graph paper to complete this homework.

1. The students in Room 305 write to pen pals in Phoenix, Arizona. The Arizona pen pals sent back the following data on the number of times their families have moved. Use the data to create a bar graph. Remember to label the axes and title your graph.

2. Answer the following questions using the bar graph you drew in Question 1.

   A. Is the variable on your horizontal axis numerical or categorical?

   B. Is the variable on your vertical axis numerical or categorical?

   C. What is the most common number of times students moved?

   D. What is the most number of times any student moved?

   E. Describe the shape of your graph.

3. What does the graph tell you about the Phoenix pen pals?

Number of Times Families Moved

Number of Times Moved M	Number of Students S
0	0
1	3
2	7
3	7
4	3
5	2
6	2
7	2
8	1
9	1
10	0

Finding the Median

Mr. Moreno's class was collecting data on the heights of fifth graders. Mr. Moreno asked Dr. Solinas to talk to the class about how children grow and develop. One of the things Dr. Solinas talked about was the average height of eleven-year-olds. What does "average" mean?

- "It was just an average day."
- "The doctor said my height is above average for kids my age."
- "We really need rain. Rainfall this year has been well below average."
- "My average grade in spelling is 75 percent."
- "Our soccer team averages about three goals per game."

Each sentence describes what is usual or typical for the situation.

Scientists and mathematicians use averages to help them describe data they collect. Doctors, who study how children grow, measure the heights of many children. Then they use this data to find the average height for different age groups. They use one number, an **average,** to represent the data from a whole group.

The average value for any set of numbers, such as the average height of fifth graders, can be calculated in more than one way. In Lesson 1 you learned about one kind of average: the mode. In this lesson you will learn about another kind of average: the median. You can find the median of a set of numbers easily and use it to describe the data you collect. Later this year, you will learn to calculate a third kind of average: the mean.

Blackline Master

The **median** is the number that is exactly in the middle of a set of data. Mr. Moreno asked five students to stand in front of the room to show the class how to find medians. Edward, Ana, Alexis, Roberto, and Shannon stood in a line from shortest to tallest. The median height of the 5 students is the height of the person exactly in the middle.

Discuss

1. **A.** Which student has the median height in the group above?

   B. Does it make sense to say this student's height is the "typical" height for this group? Why or why not?

2. **A.** Use the information in the table to find the median height for Brandon's group. Put the numbers in order from smallest to largest. The median height will be in the middle of the data.

   B. After you find the median, look back at the data. An average is one number that can be used to represent all the data. Does your answer make sense?

Brandon's Group: Our Heights

Name	Height in Inches
Brandon	55 in
Nila	51 in
John	57 in
Michael	55 in
Blanca	58 in
Jackie	54 in
Lee Yah	53 in

3. Brandon, Arti, Jessie, and Shannon all walk to school together.

- Brandon lives 1 block from school.
- Arti lives 4 blocks from school.
- Jessie lives 7 blocks from school.
- Shannon lives 2 blocks from school.

To find the median, Jessie found the number halfway between the middle two values. Jessie said, "The median number of blocks that the four of us walk to school is 3 blocks." Why do you think this is correct?

4. Use the information in the data table at the right to find the median number of blocks the students in Manny's group live from school.

5. Look at Room 305's data and graph.
 A. Find the median number of blocks.
 B. Explain how you found the median.

Manny's Group: Number of Blocks We Live from School

Name	Number of Blocks from School
Manny	2
John	1
Felicia	3
Michael	8
Frank	5
Blanca	2

Room 305: Number of Blocks We Live from School

Number of Blocks B	Tally	Number of Students S
1	///	3
2	//// //	7
3	////	4
4	//	2
5	/	1
6		0
7	/	1
8	////	4

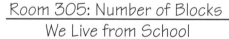

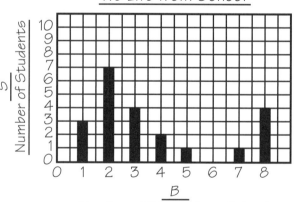

Room 305: Number of Blocks We Live from School

Explore

6. The students in Room 305 collected data on the number of times their families had moved. Here is the data for Lin's group. Find the median number of times the students in her group moved.

7. Edward's baseball team played eight games. Here are the number of runs they scored: 1, 3, 5, 3, 2, 7, 2, 4. Find the median number of runs they scored.

Lin's Group: Number of Times We Moved

Name	Number of Times Moved
Lin	2
Irma	1
Nicholas	5
Romesh	0
Manny	3

Homework

1. Romesh took a survey on his block and recorded his data in a table. Find the median number of pets on his block.

2. Ana and her two brothers play soccer. They all play on different teams. Find the median number of goals for each team.

   A. Ana's team played 6 games. Here are the number of goals her team scored in the six games: 4, 4, 0, 3, 2, 5.

   B. David's team played 5 games. Here are the number of goals his team scored: 2, 1, 3, 2, 3.

   C. Tony's team played 4 games. Here are the number of goals his team scored: 1, 0, 3, 6.

   D. Ana claims that her team is the best. Do you agree? Why or why not?

Romesh's Pets Survey

Family	Number of Pets
Bailey	2
Johnson	0
Cruz	5
Kanno	3
Holt	4
Elkins	1
Roberts	2

Name _____   Date _____

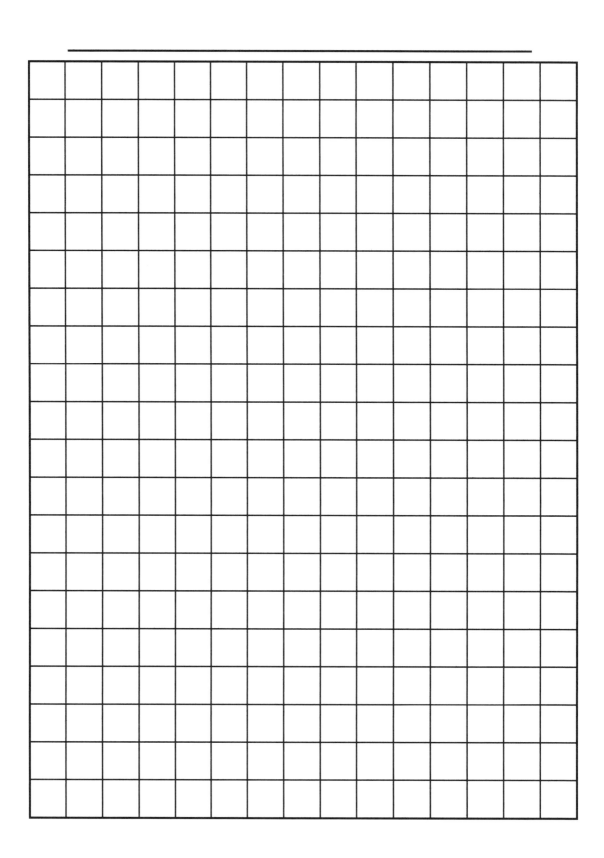

Centimeter Graph Paper, Blackline Master

_____

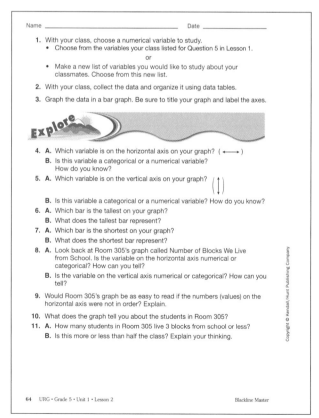

Unit Resource Guide - page 63

Name _____ Date _____

1. With your class, choose a numerical variable to study.
   • Choose from the variables your class listed for Question 5 in Lesson 1.
     or
   • Make a new list of variables you would like to study about your classmates. Choose from this new list.
2. With your class, collect the data and organize it using data tables.
3. Graph the data in a bar graph. Be sure to title your graph and label the axes.

Explore

4. **A.** Which variable is on the horizontal axis on your graph? (⟷)
   B. Is this variable a categorical or a numerical variable? How do you know?
5. **A.** Which variable is on the vertical axis on your graph? (↕)
   B. Is this variable a categorical or a numerical variable? How do you know?
6. **A.** Which bar is the tallest on your graph?
   B. What does the tallest bar represent?
7. **A.** Which bar is the shortest on your graph?
   B. What does the shortest bar represent?
8. **A.** Look back at Room 305's graph called Number of Blocks We Live from School. Is the variable on the horizontal axis numerical or categorical? How can you tell?
   B. Is the variable on the vertical axis numerical or categorical? How can you tell?
9. Would Room 305's graph be as easy to read if the numbers (values) on the horizontal axis were not in order? Explain.
10. What does the graph tell you about the students in Room 305?
11. **A.** How many students in Room 305 live 3 blocks from school or less?
    B. Is this more or less than half the class? Explain your thinking.

64   URG • Grade 5 • Unit 1 • Lesson 2   Blackline Master

Unit Resource Guide - page 64

Unit Resource Guide (pp. 63–64)

Collecting, Organizing, and Graphing Data

1. Answers will vary.*

2. See Figures 5 and 6 in Lesson Guide 2 for sample data tables.*

3. See Figure 7 in Lesson Guide 2 for a sample graph.*

The answers to *Questions 4–7* are based on the data in Figures 6 and 7 in Lesson Guide 2.

4. **A.** Number of Pets
   B. Numerical; the values are numbers.

5. **A.** Number of Students
   B. Numerical; the values are numbers.

6. **A.** 2 pets
   B. 2 pets is the most common number of pets. (This is the mode.)

7. **A.** 4 and 6 pets
   B. 4 pets and 6 pets are the least common number of pets.

8. **A.** numerical
   B. numerical

9. No; The shape of the graph tells us more when the values are in order.*

10. The majority of the students in Room 305 live near school—3 blocks or closer. Not as many students live between 5 and 7 blocks away. Then the final bar shows that a few students live quite far. These students might get to school by bus.*

11. **A.** 14 students
    B. More than half; there are 22 students in all. 14 is more than half of 22.

*Answers and/or discussion are included in the Lesson Guide.

Unit Resource Guide (p. 65)

Homework

1.

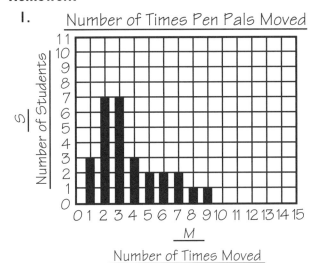

Number of Times Pen Pals Moved

(graph: Number of Students (S) on vertical axis, Number of Times Moved (M) on horizontal axis)

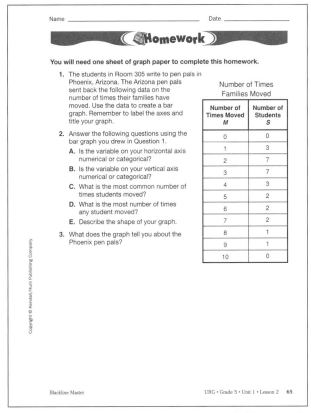

Unit Resource Guide - page 65

2. **A.** numerical

   B. numerical

   C. One bar shows that seven students moved twice. Another bar shows that seven students moved three times. These two bars represent the most common number of times students have moved—2 or 3 times.

   D. 9 times

   E. Answers will vary. There are 9 bars on the graphs. The bars at the beginning of the graph are taller than the bars at the end. The tallest bars are for a small number of moves. The shortest bars are for a large number of moves.

3. Answers will vary. It is most common for a student in the Phoenix classroom to have moved 2 or 3 times. Every student has moved at least once since there is no bar for zero moves. Most students have moved 3 times or less since the tallest bars are at the beginning. The short bars at the end tell us that a few students have moved many times.

Name _____ Date _____

Finding the Median

Mr. Moreno's class was collecting data on the heights of fifth graders. Mr. Moreno asked Dr. Solinas to talk to the class about how children grow and develop. One of the things Dr. Solinas talked about was the average height of eleven-year-olds. What does "average" mean?

- "It was just an average day."
- "The doctor said my height is above average for kids my age."
- "We really need rain. Rainfall this year has been well below average."
- "My average grade in spelling is 75 percent."
- "Our soccer team averages about three goals per game."

Each sentence describes what is usual or typical for the situation.

Scientists and mathematicians use averages to help them describe data they collect. Doctors, who study how children grow, measure the heights of many children. Then they use this data to find the average height for different age groups. They use one number, an **average,** to represent the data from a whole group.

The average value for any set of numbers, such as the average height of fifth graders, can be calculated in more than one way. In Lesson 1 you learned about one kind of average: the mode. In this lesson you will learn about another kind of average: the median. You can find the median of a set of numbers easily and use it to describe the data you collect. Later this year, you will learn to calculate a third kind of average: the mean.

66   URG • Grade 5 • Unit 1 • Lesson 2   Blackline Master

Unit Resource Guide - page 66

Unit Resource Guide (pp. 66–67)

Finding the Median

1.* A. Alexis

   B. Yes. Alexis is not the tallest or the shortest; her height is in the middle.

2. A. 55 inches

   B. Yes

Name _____ Date _____

The **median** is the number that is exactly in the middle of a set of data. Mr. Moreno asked five students to stand in front of the room to show the class how to find medians. Edward, Ana, Alexis, Roberto, and Shannon stood in a line from shortest to tallest. The median height of the 5 students is the height of the person exactly in the middle.

Discuss

1. A. Which student has the median height in the group above?

   B. Does it make sense to say this student's height is the "typical" height for this group? Why or why not?

2. A. Use the information in the table to find the median height for Brandon's group. Put the numbers in order from smallest to largest. The median height will be in the middle of the data.

   B. After you find the median, look back at the data. An average is one number that can be used to represent all the data. Does your answer make sense?

Brandon's Group: Our Heights

Name	Height in Inches
Brandon	55 in
Nila	51 in
John	57 in
Michael	55 in
Blanca	58 in
Jackie	54 in
Lee Yah	53 in

Blackline Master   URG • Grade 5 • Unit 1 • Lesson 2   67

Unit Resource Guide - page 67

*Answers and/or discussion are included in the Lesson Guide.

Unit Resource Guide (p. 68)

3. Yes, 3 is halfway between 2 and 4.

4. $2\frac{1}{2}$ blocks

5.* A. 3 blocks

   B. Answers may vary. Students might use the data table or graph to find the median. For example, students can count off each tally mark in the data table, one at the top of the table and one at the bottom, until they reach the center. See Figure 9 in Lesson Guide 2. Students can also use the graph in a similar way.

Unit Resource Guide - page 68

Unit Resource Guide (p. 69)

6. 2 moves

7. 3 runs

Homework

1. 2 pets

2. A. 3.5 goals

   B. 2 goals

   C. 2 goals

   D. Answers will vary. Students may feel that Ana's team is the best because her median number of goals (3.5 goals) is the highest or students may feel that Tony's team is the best because his team has the highest number of goals in all of the games (6 goals).

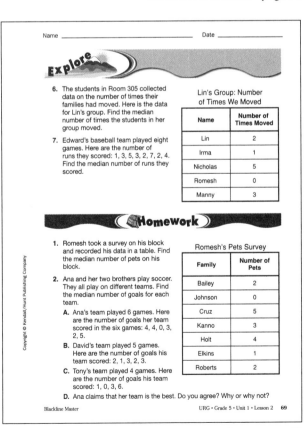

Unit Resource Guide - page 69

Lesson 3

Analyzing Data

Lesson Overview

Estimated Class Sessions

1

This lesson has two parts. In the first part, students compare and analyze data in graphs. In the second part, they review using averages to represent data. In this lesson they concentrate on the mode and median.

Key Content

- Translating between graphs and real-world events.
- Averaging: finding the median.
- Identifying the mode.

Key Vocabulary

- mean
- median
- mode

Math Facts

Use the Addition and Subtraction Math Facts Review section of the *Facts Resource Guide* as needed.

Homework

1. Assign the Homework section in the *Student Guide.*
2. Assign Part 3 of the Home Practice in the *Discovery Assignment Book.*

Assessment

Use *Question 1* in the Homework section as an assessment.

Curriculum Sequence

Before This Unit

Analyzing Graphs

Students using *Math Trailblazers* have had many experiences analyzing graphs in earlier grades. Three examples from the fourth-grade curriculum follow: they drew best-fit lines to make predictions about winning times in future Olympics in Unit 5, they used the shape of bar graphs to analyze the data in a probability experiment in Unit 14, and they investigated the growth curves of young plants in Unit 15.

Medians

Beginning in first grade, students used medians to analyze data collected in labs. In fourth grade, they reviewed the use of medians to represent data in Unit 1 Lesson 3 *An Average Activity,* and they compared the use of the median to the mean in Unit 5 Lesson 2 *Another Average Activity.*

After This Unit

Analyzing Graphs

Students will continue to analyze graphs as part of labs. For example, they will use line graphs to compare the speeds of students running and walking in the lab *A Day at the Races* in Unit 5, and they will again use bar graphs to analyze data in a probability experiment in the lab *Flipping Two Coins* in Unit 7.

Medians

Using the median to average data will continue throughout fifth grade. Students will also review the use of the mean to represent data in Unit 4.

Materials List

Supplies and Copies

Student	Teacher
Supplies for Each Student	**Supplies**
Copies	**Copies/Transparencies**

All blackline masters including assessment, transparency, and DPP masters are also on the Teacher Resource CD.

Student Books
Analyzing Data (*Student Guide* Pages 10–16)

Daily Practice and Problems and Home Practice
DPP items G–H (*Unit Resource Guide* Pages 20–21)
Home Practice Part 3 (*Discovery Assignment Book* Page 4)

Note: Classrooms whose pacing differs significantly from the suggested pacing of the units should use the Math Facts Calendar in Section 4 of the *Facts Resource Guide* to ensure students receive the complete math facts program.

Daily Practice and Problems

Suggestions for using the DPPs are on page 83.

G. Bit: Purchasing Shoes (URG p. 20)

Alexander is purchasing a pair of shoes for $23.95 and two new pairs of socks at $1.25 each.

1. How much is Alexander's purchase without tax?
2. With tax, Alexander owes the sales clerk $28.30. About how much was the tax?
3. If Alexander gives the clerk $30.00, how much change should he receive?

H. Task: What's for Lunch? (URG p. 21)

Mr. Moreno's class went on a field trip to the museum. They went to lunch in the museum cafeteria. Shannon collected the following data about what her classmates ate for lunch.

Type of Food	Number of Students
Tacos	3
Pizza	10
Hamburgers	15
Chicken	2

1. Make a bar graph of Shannon's data on graph paper.
2. What variable did you graph on the horizontal axis?
3. What variable did you graph on the vertical axis?
4. Identify each variable as categorical or numerical.
5. What are some questions you could answer using the graph?

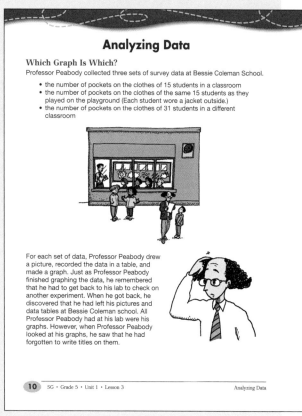

Analyzing Data

Which Graph Is Which?
Professor Peabody collected three sets of survey data at Bessie Coleman School.

- the number of pockets on the clothes of 15 students in a classroom
- the number of pockets on the clothes of the same 15 students as they played on the playground (Each student wore a jacket outside.)
- the number of pockets on the clothes of 31 students in a different classroom

For each set of data, Professor Peabody drew a picture, recorded the data in a table, and made a graph. Just as Professor Peabody finished graphing the data, he remembered that he had to get back to his lab to check on another experiment. When he got back, he discovered that he had left his pictures and data tables at Bessie Coleman school. All Professor Peabody had at his lab were his graphs. However, when Professor Peabody looked at his graphs, he saw that he had forgotten to write titles on them.

Analyzing Data

Student Guide - page 10 (Answers on p. 86)

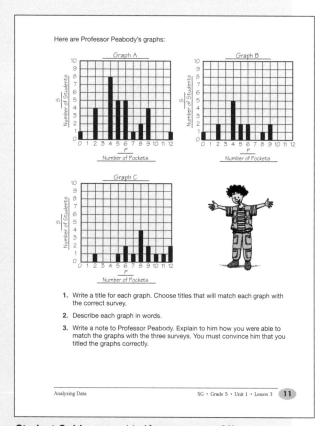

Here are Professor Peabody's graphs:

1. Write a title for each graph. Choose titles that will match each graph with the correct survey.

2. Describe each graph in words.

3. Write a note to Professor Peabody. Explain to him how you were able to match the graphs with the three surveys. You must convince him that you titled the graphs correctly.

Student Guide - page 11 (Answers on p. 86)

Teaching the Activity

Part 1 **Which Graph Is Which?**

To begin this activity, read the description of Professor Peabody's problem on the *Analyzing Data* Activity Pages in the *Student Guide*. The professor has collected survey data on the number of pockets on the clothes of three groups of students, but he has lost his data tables and he forgot to title the three graphs. Students must match the graphs to the descriptions of each survey and write a title for each *(Question 1)*.

In *Question 2* students write a description of each graph. Encourage them to use the same language they used in Lesson 1 when they described the Eyelets graphs. Use the following prompts to help them write about the shape of the graph:

- *Are all the bars about the same height?*
- *Are some bars taller than others? Where are the taller bars?*
- *Which bar is the tallest bar?*
- *Are the bars spread out?*
- *Are they close together? If so, where are they located on the graph?*

Question 3 asks students to write a note to Professor Peabody explaining how they matched the graphs to the three sets of data. Using the descriptions, they should compare the graphs and relate the shapes of the graphs to the three populations in the data collection. The shapes of all three graphs are similar. One tall bar is surrounded by shorter bars. However, since the bars on Graph A are taller than the bars on Graphs B and C, Graph A represents more students and might be titled, "Number of Pockets on 31 Students in Class." The bars on Graph C are to the right of the bars on Graph B. Note that the mode (the tallest bar) in Graph C has shifted from 4 pockets on Graph B to 8 pockets on Graph C. This tells us that Graph C represents more pockets. So, Graph C might be titled, "Pockets of 15 Students on the Playground" (students on the playground wear jackets, so they had more pockets). Graph B can be titled, "Pockets of 15 Students in Class."

The questions and the text in the Reviewing Averages section in the *Student Guide* review the use of averages to represent data, in particular, the mode and the median. The text on page 13 provides an example of the procedure for finding the median of a set of data with an odd number of values and an example for finding the median of a set of data with an even number of values. (See Content Note.)

Content Note

Average. In everyday language we use average to describe what is normal or typical. In mathematics, the **average** is a single value that is used to represent a set of numbers. For example, the average grade for a student is one number that is used to represent all of his or her grades. In fifth grade, we review the median in this unit and the mean in Unit 4. The mode is a third kind of average. It was introduced in Lesson 1 and is discussed again in this lesson.

The arithmetic **mean** is the most commonly used average. If a student spells 18, 19, 10, 14, and 19 words correctly on a series of five spelling tests, the student's mean number correct is (18 + 19 + 10 + 14 + 19) ÷ 5 which equals 16. The **mode** is the most common value, so the mode for this set of data is 19.

The **median** is the number exactly in the middle of the scores. To find the median of an odd number of scores, arrange the scores from smallest to largest and choose the middle number. The median score for the above data (10, 14, 18, 19, 19) is 18 since there are two values smaller than 18 and two values larger than 18. If a student takes an even number of tests, the median is not as obvious since there is not one middle piece of data. If a student earns scores of 10, 14, 18, and 19 on four tests, his or her median score is 16. In this case, we look at the two middle pieces of data (14 and 18) and the median is the number halfway between these two numbers (16). If a student earns scores of 10, 13, 18, and 19 on the four tests, the median score is 15.5, since it is midway between 13 and 18. (See the TIMS Tutor: *Averages* in the *Teacher Implementation Guide* for more detailed information on the different types of averages including a discussion on the appropriate uses of each.)

The questions in the *Student Guide* provide practice finding the median and mode. Some questions ask students to make decisions on the appropriate use of averages to represent a data set. For example, the data discussed in *Question 5* is shown in Figure 10.

Reviewing Averages
A graph is a good way to represent a set of data since it gives us a picture of *all* the data. Another way to represent a set of data is to find an **average.** An average is one number that can be used to represent a set of data.

There is more than one way to find an average. The **mode** is one kind of average. In Lesson 1, you learned that the mode is the most common value in a set of data.

4. Find the mode for each set of survey data represented by a graph in Question 1.

5. Professor Peabody returned to Bessie Coleman School to get his pictures and data tables. While he was there, he collected data on the number of pockets the teachers had.
   A. What is the mode for the data in the table below?
   B. Does it make sense to say this number of pockets is typical for the teachers? Why or why not?

Teachers' Pockets

Teacher	Number of Pockets
Mrs. Dewey	1
Mr. Martinez	6
Mrs. Lee	0
Mr. Green	6
Mrs. Scott	2
Mrs. Grace	3
Mrs. Sharma	4

12 SG • Grade 5 • Unit 1 • Lesson 3   Analyzing Data

Student Guide - page 12 *(Answers on p. 87)*

Teachers' Pockets

Teacher	Number of Pockets
Mrs. Dewey	1
Mr. Martinez	6
Mrs. Lee	0
Mr. Green	6
Mrs. Scott	2
Mrs. Grace	3
Mrs. Sharma	4

Figure 10: *Data table for* Question 5 *in the* Student Guide

The **median** is another kind of average. You have used the median to average data in labs or other activities. It is the number that is exactly in the middle of the data. For example, to find the median of the number of teachers' pockets, you can list the numbers in order from smallest to largest like this.

0, 1, 2, ③, 4, 6, 6

Since 3 is exactly in the middle of the data, 3 pockets is the median.

6. Which average, the median or the mode, do you think represents the Teachers' Pockets data better? Tell why.

Here is another example. Professor Peabody found the height of six teachers. He found the median as shown.

Teachers' Heights

Teacher	Height in Inches
Mrs. Dewey	66
Mr. Martinez	70
Mrs. Lee	60
Mr. Green	72
Mrs. Scott	62
Mrs. Sharma	61

60 inches, 61 inches, 62 inches, 66 inches, 70 inches, 72 inches

↑
(64 inches)

The median height is 64 inches, since it is exactly in the middle of the data. (It is halfway between 62 inches and 66 inches.)

Student Guide - page 13 (Answers on p. 87)

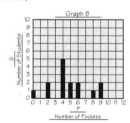

The **mean** is a third kind of average. When people talk about averages in everyday life, they usually are talking about the mean. We will review the mean in a later unit.

7. **A.** Find the median of the data in Graph B. (*Hint:* How many students are represented in the graph? What number of pockets is exactly in the middle of the data?)

B. Are the median and the mode the same for this set of data?

8. Fruit Gem Snacks come in three sizes. Arti and Jessie wanted to know how many fruit gems come in each size bag. They counted the number of fruit gems in three bags of each size and recorded the data in this table. Find the median number of fruit gems in each size bag.

Size	Number of Fruit Gems			
	Bag 1	Bag 2	Bag 3	Median
Small	10	12	11	
Medium	18	18	16	
Big Snack	25	27	24	

Student Guide - page 14 (Answers on p. 88)

In **Question 5A,** students identify the mode as 6 pockets, since 6 is the most common value in the table (it occurs twice). **Question 5B** asks if it makes sense to say that 6 pockets is typical for the teachers. Since the values range from 0 pockets to 6 pockets and most of the teachers have fewer than 5 pockets, 6 pockets does not represent the data very well. **Question 5** is followed by an explanation of the procedure for finding the median number of pockets. Since 3 is exactly in the middle of the data, 3 pockets is the median value. **Question 6** asks which average, the median or the mode, represents the data better. The median does a better job since it is more typical of the complete data set.

Question 7 asks students to find the median of the data represented in Graph B in the *Student Guide*. Figure 11 is a copy of this graph. They can pull the values in the data set from the graph, list them in order, and then choose the middle value.

0, 2, 2, 4, 4, 4, 4, ④, 5, 5, 6, 6, 8, 9, 9

Students can also use the graph to find the median as shown in Figure 11. They count off each piece of data from both ends of the graph until they reach the middle value. This piece of data is circled in Figure 11. The median is 4 pockets, since the middle value falls on the bar for 4 pockets.

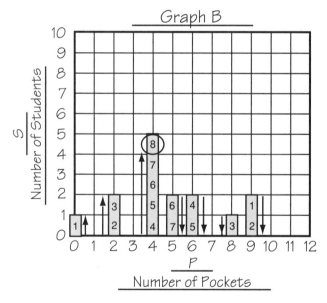

Figure 11: *Graph for* Question 7 *in the Student Guide*

Students find the average (median) of 3 students' spelling scores in **Question 9A.** In **Question 9B,** students must choose the best speller. Answers may vary, but students must make logical arguments to justify their choices. For example, Lin may be recognized as the best speller since her median score is the highest (9). However, either Grace or Luis could be named the best speller since their median scores are both 8, and they are more consistent than Lin. Note that students familiar with finding the mean may include the means of students in their arguments. As you discuss this question, point out that it is often not possible to draw absolute conclusions about a data set.

Homework and Practice

- The Homework section in the *Student Guide* provides another group of graphs to analyze and more practice with medians and modes.

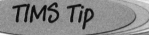

TIMS Tip

To answer **Question 1** in the Homework section, students need to recognize reasonable heights for fifth graders. You may ask several students how tall they are before assigning the homework. Or you may ask two or three students to measure their heights (in inches) and report the results to the class.

- Assign Task H from the Daily Practice and Problems for practice making bar graphs and identifying numerical and categorical variables.
- Assign Part 3 of the Home Practice in the *Discovery Assignment Book* for more practice finding medians.

Answers for Part 3 of the Home Practice are in the Answer Key at the end of this lesson and at the end of this unit.

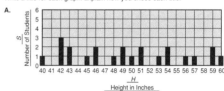

9. Lin, Jacob, Grace, and Luis are in four different fifth-grade classrooms. Each class gives spelling quizzes with 10 words. Their spelling scores are listed below:

Lin: 10, 4, 9, 10, 8
Jacob: 8, 9, 8, 6, 5, 6
Grace: 7, 8, 8, 9, 8, 10
Luis: 8, 8, 8, 8, 8

A. Find the median spelling score for each student.
B. Who do you think is the best speller? Explain your thinking.

Homework

Mr. Moreno's fifth-grade class collected three sets of data:

- the heights of the students in Mr. Moreno's fifth-grade class
- the heights of a class of kindergarten students
- the heights of 23 students in the school cafeteria at lunch time (Students in kindergarten through fifth grade eat lunch together.)

1. They made a graph for each set of data. These graphs are shown here. Write a title for each graph. Explain how you chose each title.

A.

Analyzing Data   SG • Grade 5 • Unit 1 • Lesson 3   **15**

Student Guide - page 15 (Answers on p. 88)

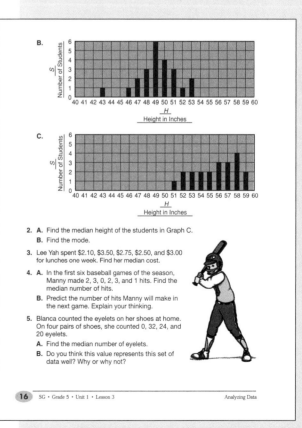

B.

C.

2. **A.** Find the median height of the students in Graph C.
   B. Find the mode.

3. Lee Yah spent $2.10, $3.50, $2.75, $2.50, and $3.00 for lunches one week. Find her median cost.

4. **A.** In the first six baseball games of the season, Manny made 2, 3, 0, 2, 3, and 1 hits. Find the median number of hits.
   B. Predict the number of hits Manny will make in the next game. Explain your thinking.

5. Blanca counted the eyelets on her shoes at home. On four pairs of shoes, she counted 0, 32, 24, and 20 eyelets.
   A. Find the median number of eyelets.
   B. Do you think this value represents this set of data well? Why or why not?

16   SG • Grade 5 • Unit 1 • Lesson 3   Analyzing Data

Student Guide - page 16 (Answers on p. 89)

Assessment

Use *Question 1* in the Homework section to assess students' abilities to analyze data in a graph and communicate their mathematical reasoning.

Extension

Choose a numerical variable to study from your data table of variables and values the class generated in Lesson 1. Collect and graph data from three different populations. For example, one population can be larger than the other two and one population can be younger or older. Compare and analyze the graphs from the three populations using the discussion prompts in Part 1 of this Lesson Guide.

Journal Prompt

A stream has an average depth of 1 meter. Can you wade across?

At a Glance

Math Facts and Daily Practice and Problems

Assign Bit G from the Daily Practice and Problems to provide practice with mental math and estimation strategies and Task H for practice with graphing and identifying variables.

Part 1. Which Graph Is Which?

1. Read and discuss Professor Peabody's problem as described in the first part of the *Analyzing Data* Activity Pages in the *Student Guide.*
2. Students match three descriptions of three sets of survey data with three graphs. They write titles for each graph, describe each graph in words, and justify their choices. *(Questions 1–3)*

Part 2. Reviewing Averages

1. Students review the use of averages (median and mode) to represent data by reading the Reviewing Averages section of the *Student Guide.*
2. Students solve problems involving medians and modes. *(Questions 4–9)*

Homework

1. Assign the Homework section in the *Student Guide.*
2. Assign Part 3 of the Home Practice in the *Discovery Assignment Book.*

Assessment

Use *Question 1* in the Homework section as an assessment.

Extension

Have students choose a numerical variable to study. They then collect and graph the data from three different populations and compare the results.

Answer Key is on pages 86–89.

Notes:

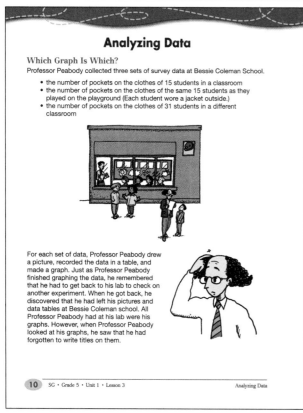

Student Guide - page 10

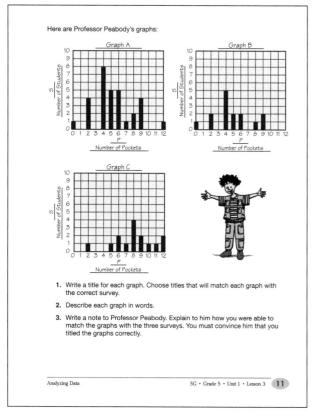

Student Guide - page 11

*Answers and/or discussion are included in the Lesson Guide.

Student Guide (pp. 10–11)

1. Titles will vary. Graph A: Pockets on 31 Students Inside. Graph B: Pockets on 15 Students Inside. Graph C: Pockets on 15 Students Outside.

2. Descriptions will vary. Possible descriptions include: Since the bars are spread out, Graph A shows students wearing clothes with numbers of pockets ranging from 0 to 12. The bars are different heights with the tallest bars around 4 pockets and the shortest bars at each end. The bars are taller than on Graphs B and C. The shape of Graph B is similar to the shape of Graph A, but the bars are shorter. No students are wearing clothes with 10 or more pockets. The tallest bar is the bar for 4 pockets. Graph C has a similar shape, but the bars have moved to the right side of the graph. The tallest bar is the bar for 8 pockets. Most students are wearing clothes with 8 or more pockets while no students are wearing clothes with 0 or 1 pocket.*

3. Notes will vary. Some possible arguments include: Since Graph A has taller bars, it represents more students. It represents 31 students. The remaining two graphs describe the students in the same classroom, one with jackets, the other without. Since jackets usually have pockets, the graph that shows more pockets is the one that is outside. Since the bars on Graph C are to the right of Graph B, Graph C represents more pockets. So Graph C is titled "Pockets on 15 Students Outside" and Graph B is titled "Pockets of 15 Students Inside."*

Student Guide (p. 12)

4. Graph A: 4 pockets. Graph B: 4 pockets. Graph C: 8 pockets.

5.* **A.** 6 pockets

B. Answers will vary. Not really, the data show that 6 is the most number of pockets in the data and only 2 teachers have 6 pockets. It does not represent the center of the data.

Reviewing Averages

A graph is a good way to represent a set of data since it gives us a picture of *all* the data. Another way to represent a set of data is to find an **average**. An average is one number that can be used to represent a set of data.

There is more than one way to find an average. The **mode** is one kind of average. In Lesson 1, you learned that the mode is the most common value in a set of data.

4. Find the mode for each set of survey data represented by a graph in Question 1.

5. Professor Peabody returned to Bessie Coleman School to get his pictures and data tables. While he was there, he collected data on the number of pockets the teachers had.

A. What is the mode for the data in the table below?

B. Does it make sense to say this number of pockets is typical for the teachers? Why or why not?

Teachers' Pockets

Teacher	Number of Pockets
Mrs. Dewey	1
Mr. Martinez	6
Mrs. Lee	0
Mr. Green	6
Mrs. Scott	2
Mrs. Grace	3
Mrs. Sharma	4

12 SG • Grade 5 • Unit 1 • Lesson 3   Analyzing Data

Student Guide - page 12

Student Guide (p. 13)

6. Answers will vary. The median is a better average. It shows that some teachers have less than 3 pockets and some have more.*

The **median** is another kind of average. You have used the median to average data in labs or other activities. It is the number that is exactly in the middle of the data. For example, to find the median of the number of teachers' pockets, you can list the numbers in order from smallest to largest like this.

0, 1, 2, ③, 4, 6, 6

Since 3 is exactly in the middle of the data, 3 pockets is the median.

6. Which average, the median or the mode, do you think represents the Teachers' Pockets data better? Tell why.

Here is another example. Professor Peabody found the height of six teachers. He found the median as shown.

Teachers' Heights

Teacher	Height in Inches
Mrs. Dewey	66
Mr. Martinez	70
Mrs. Lee	60
Mr. Green	72
Mrs. Scott	62
Mrs. Sharma	61

60 inches, 61 inches, 62 inches, 66 inches, 70 inches, 72 inches

64 inches

The median height is 64 inches, since it is exactly in the middle of the data. (It is halfway between 62 inches and 66 inches.)

Analyzing Data   SG • Grade 5 • Unit 1 • Lesson 3 **13**

Student Guide - page 13

---

*Answers and/or discussion are included in the Lesson Guide.

The **mean** is a third kind of average. When people talk about averages in everyday life, they usually are talking about the mean. We will review the mean in a later unit.

7. A. Find the median of the data in Graph B. (*Hint:* How many students are represented in the graph? What number of pockets is exactly in the middle of the data?)

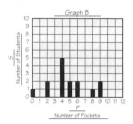

Graph B

B. Are the median and the mode the same for this set of data?

8. Fruit Gem Snacks come in three sizes. Arti and Jessie wanted to know how many fruit gems come in each size bag. They counted the number of fruit gems in three bags of each size and recorded the data in this table. Find the median number of fruit gems in each size bag.

Size	Number of Fruit Gems			
	Bag 1	Bag 2	Bag 3	Median
Small	10	12	11	
Medium	18	18	16	
Big Snack	25	27	24	

Student Guide - page 14

9. Lin, Jacob, Grace, and Luis are in four different fifth-grade classrooms. Each class gives spelling quizzes with 10 words. Their spelling scores are listed below:

Lin: 10, 4, 9, 10, 8
Jacob: 8, 9, 8, 6, 5, 6
Grace: 7, 8, 8, 9, 8, 10
Luis: 8, 8, 8, 8, 8

A. Find the median spelling score for each student.
B. Who do you think is the best speller? Explain your thinking.

Homework

Mr. Moreno's fifth-grade class collected three sets of data:

- the heights of the students in Mr. Moreno's fifth-grade class
- the heights of a class of kindergarten students
- the heights of 23 students in the school cafeteria at lunch time (Students in kindergarten through fifth grade eat lunch together.)

1. They made a graph for each set of data. These graphs are shown here. Write a title for each graph. Explain how you chose each title.

A.

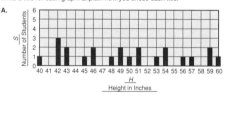

Height in Inches

Student Guide - page 15

---

7. A. 4 pockets*

B. Yes

8. Small: 11 gems. Medium: 18 gems. Big snack: 25 gems.

9. A. Lin: 9. Jacob: 7. Grace: 8. Luis: 8.

B. Answers will vary. One possible solution is that Lin is the best speller since she has the highest median or has two high scores of 10.

Homework

1. Titles will vary. Graph A: Heights of 23 Students at Lunch Time. This graph shows a wide range of heights and represents 23 students. Graph B: Heights of Kindergartners. This graph shows students who are shorter than the students in Graph C since most of the bars in Graph B are to the left of the bars in Graph C. Graph C: Heights of Fifth Graders. This graph shows heights taller than Graph B (since the bars are to the right), so it must be the height of the fifth graders in Mr. Moreno's class. Also, students should recognize the heights represented by this graph (51 inches to 59 inches) as reasonable heights for fifth graders.

*Answers and/or discussion are included in the Lesson Guide.

Student Guide (p. 16)

Homework

2. A. Median: 56 inches

B. Mode: 58 inches

3. $2.75

4. A. 2 hits

B. Predictions will vary. A good prediction is 2 hits since that is his median number of hits. Any predictions greater than 3 hits would not make sense, since Manny has never made that many hits.

5. A. 22 eyelets

B. Explanations will vary. One possible solution is to say, "no," since the median value is not an actual value of the number of eyelets on a pair of shoes.

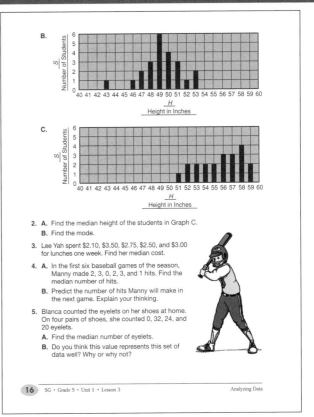

2. A. Find the median height of the students in Graph C.
B. Find the mode.

3. Lee Yah spent $2.10, $3.50, $2.75, $2.50, and $3.00 for lunches one week. Find her median cost.

4. A. In the first six baseball games of the season, Manny made 2, 3, 0, 2, 3, and 1 hits. Find the median number of hits.
B. Predict the number of hits Manny will make in the next game. Explain your thinking.

5. Blanca counted the eyelets on her shoes at home. On four pairs of shoes, she counted 0, 32, 24, and 20 eyelets.
A. Find the median number of eyelets.
B. Do you think this value represents this set of data well? Why or why not?

16   SG • Grade 5 • Unit 1 • Lesson 3   Analyzing Data

Student Guide - page 16

Discovery Assignment Book (p. 4)

Home Practice*

Part 3. Finding the Median

1. 18 videos

2. 24 eyelets

3. 5 pairs of shoes, 5 pairs of shoes

4. $1.45

5. Answers will vary. Everyone in the family can line up by height, then measure the middle person's height.

Name _____ Date _____

PART 3 Finding the Median
Find the median for each set of data given below. Show how you decided.

1. Roberto, David, Nila, Lee Yah, and Romesh compared the number of videos their families own. Roberto owns 47 videos while David only owns 4. Nila owns 23 videos, Lee Yah owns 18 videos, and Romesh owns 15 videos. What is the median number of videos? (*Hint:* First list the number of videos owned by each family in order from smallest to largest. You should list five numbers.)

2. Brandon compared five different types of basketball shoes. His favorite brand has 24 eyelets. His least favorite has 32 eyelets. Two brands have pairs of shoes with 20 eyelets. Another brand has 28 eyelets. What is the median number of eyelets? (*Hint:* List the number 20 twice since two pairs of shoes have 20 eyelets.)

3. There are seven people in Felicia's family. Four members of her family have 5 pairs of shoes. Two members of her family have 3 pairs of shoes. Her mother has 15 pairs of shoes. What is the median number of pairs of shoes in Felicia's household? What is the mode? (*Hint:* List the number 5 four times since four members have 5 pairs of shoes. List the number 3 twice.)

4. Four people in David's family celebrate birthdays in September. David buys 4 cards. The card for his mother costs $2.25. The cards for his two brothers are $1.25 and $1.40. The card for his cousin is $1.50. What is the median price of the birthday cards?

5. What is the median height in your household? How did you decide?

4   DAB • Grade 5 • Unit 1   POPULATIONS AND SAMPLES

Discovery Assignment Book - page 4

*Answers for all the Home Practice in the *Discovery Assignment Book* are at the end of the unit.

Lesson 4

A Matter of Survival

Lesson Overview

Estimated Class Sessions

1

This story provides an introduction to Lesson 5.

Betty Robinson and her scientist parents gather data about wildlife populations in an undisturbed region of the Amazon rain forest. The Robinsons plan to use this data to establish a baseline for evaluating the health of isolated "islands" of rain forest in other parts of the Amazon basin. The Robinsons use sampling techniques that students will apply in the lab *Searching the Forest*.

Key Content

- Sampling a population.
- Connecting mathematics and science to real-world situations.

Key Vocabulary*

- baseline
- compromise
- developed
- erosion
- isolated
- region
- reliable
- troop
- viola

Math Facts

Use the Addition and Subtraction Math Facts Review section of the *Facts Resource Guide* as needed.

Homework

Assign item I from the Daily Practice and Problems.

*Note: These words are not key mathematical vocabulary. They are, rather, words in the story that may be unfamiliar to some students.

Materials List

Supplies and Copies

Student	Teacher
Supplies for Each Student	**Supplies** • a map of South America, optional
Copies	**Copies/Transparencies**

All blackline masters including assessment, transparency, and DPP masters are also on the Teacher Resource CD.

Student Books
A Matter of Survival (*Adventure Book* Pages 1–12)

Daily Practice and Problems and Home Practice
DPP items I–J (*Unit Resource Guide* Page 22)

Note: Classrooms whose pacing differs significantly from the suggested pacing of the units should use the Math Facts Calendar in Section 4 of the *Facts Resource Guide* to ensure students receive the complete math facts program.

Daily Practice and Problems

Suggestions for using the DPPs are on page 97.

I. Bit: Skip Counting (URG p. 22)

1. List the multiples of 2 from 2 to 30. (Skip count by 2s from 2 to 30.)
2. List the multiples of 4 from 4 to 40.
3. List the multiples of 5 from 5 to 50.
4. List the multiples of 10 from 10 to 200.

J. Challenge: Counting Pennies
(URG p. 22)

Marianne counted a jug of pennies her family collected. She emptied the jug by taking ten pennies out at a time. She made a tally mark for every ten pennies. When she was finished, she had 176 tally marks.

1. How many pennies does she have?
2. How much money does Marianne have? Give your answer in dollars and cents.
3. If the pennies were exchanged for nickels, how many nickels would she have?
4. If the pennies were exchanged for dimes, how many dimes would she have?
5. If the pennies were exchanged for quarters, how many quarters would she have?

Page 1

Before you begin to read the story, ask students what they know about the Amazon rain forest. Also point out that scientists are real people with families and that students can aspire to become scientists when they grow up.

Adventure Book - page 1

Pages 3–5

This story portrays the ongoing destruction of the tropical rain forest, including the causes and potential impact. Much of the land is being converted to pasture or cropland. One theme of this story is the work scientists are doing to answer a difficult question (how to save the rain forest).

- *Why does the loss of the rain forest matter?*

Adventure Book - page 3

Adventure Book - page 4

Page 4

Loss of rain forest reduces global biodiversity due to the loss of habitat.

As the home of a variety of plant and animal species, the rain forest plays a crucial role in the planet's ecology. These species are a potential source of new medicines and other useful chemicals. Animals and plants may become extinct when suitable places to live become too scarce. Although losses of large mammals and other appealing species tend to receive the most publicity, innumerable less notable species are equally threatened, and their loss could be even more devastating.

A large amount of carbon is concentrated in rain forest vegetation. When the forest is burned, this carbon is released into the atmosphere as carbon dioxide. Some scientists fear that the ongoing rapid increases in carbon dioxide and other greenhouse gases in the atmosphere may lead to gradual climatic change.

Adventure Book - page 5

Page 5

Changes to the local ecosystem take place when rain forest is cleared. Rain forests grow on old, nutrient-poor soils. Once the forest plants are removed, the cleared land is more likely to erode or turn into desert.

Page 6

- *Why do scientists estimate wildlife populations instead of simply counting all the animals in a region equal in area to the rain forest islands?*

It is simply not practical to count all the wildlife in large regions of the Amazon rain forest; populations must be estimated by sampling. Thus the Robinsons will make as complete counts as possible in three patches, each with the same area. By assuming these patches to be representative of the entire rain forest, they can estimate how large wildlife populations ought to be in other similar known areas. Thus, they will be able to judge the health of the isolated islands of rain forest in the South.

Adventure Book - page 6

Page 9

Betty and her father are counting the number of spider monkeys in a single troop. Since there are a number of troops in each region being studied, the count for the entire region, which appears later in the story, is much larger.

Adventure Book - page 9

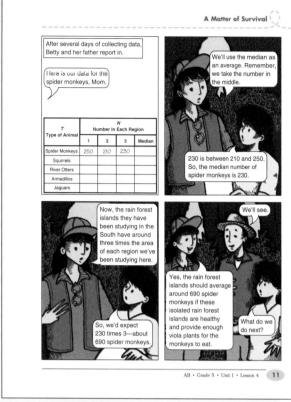

Adventure Book - page 11

Page 11

- *What variables are on the Robinsons' data table?*

Type of Animal (T) and Number in Each Region (N)

- *What values did they list for type of animal?*

Spider monkeys, squirrels, river otters, armadillos, and jaguars

- *What other variables could the Robinsons study?*

Mrs. Robinson is studying type of plants, another variable. They might also study type of insects or birds.

- *Why do the Robinsons want to find the median number for each species?*

The Robinsons use the median for their average. The median is sometimes more appropriate than the mean in population studies. (Students will review how to find the mean in Unit 4.) They are trying to get representative numbers for making predictions about the populations in the rain forest islands. By using the median, they hope to compensate for any unevenness in the distribution of the animals or errors in counting. See the TIMS Tutor: *Averages* in the *Teacher Implementation Guide* for a discussion of various kinds of averages.

- *Have you ever used any of the techniques the Robinsons use in their study?*

Students who used *Math Trailblazers* in fourth grade should be familiar with sampling, controlling variables, organizing data in tables, averaging, and making predictions from data.

Homework and Practice

Assign item I from the Daily Practice and Problems.

Extension

Assign item J for practice working with money.

Literature Connections

- Bash, Barbara. *Ancient Ones.* Sierra Club, San Francisco, 1994.
- George, Jean Craighead. *One Day in the Tropical Rain Forest.* HarperCollins, New York, 1990.
- Kipling, Rudyard. *The Jungle Books.* Bantam Books, New York, 2000.
- Yolen, Jane. *Welcome to the Green House.* Scholastic, New York, 1994.

Teaching Resource

Holloway, Marguerite. "Sustaining the Amazon." *Scientific American,* Volume 269, Number 1 (July, 1993): pp. 90–99.

Searching the Forest

Lesson Overview

Estimated Class Sessions **3**

Students use sampling to study the distribution of colors in a population of colored square-inch tiles. Students take several 10-tile samples from a bag containing 50 tiles. They record the number of tiles of each color, find the median number per sample of each color, graph the data, and analyze the results. As part of the analysis, students explore probabilities using fractions.

We recommend that you use this lab to gather baseline data on students' abilities to collect, organize, graph, and analyze data. Have students place the completed labs in their collection folders. (In Unit 2, selected items from the collection folder will be included in students' portfolios.) The Student Rubric: *Knowing* is used here to make clear the expectations of student performance.

Key Content

- Sampling a population.
- Averaging: finding the median.
- Making and interpreting bar graphs.
- Predicting population characteristics from samples.
- Collecting, organizing, graphing, and analyzing data.

Key Vocabulary

- collection folder
- median
- population
- probability
- rubric
- sample
- value
- variable

Math Facts

Use Bits K and O to assess students' fluency with the subtraction facts.

Homework

1. You can use Radio Favorites and Candy Grab in the Homework section of the *Student Guide* for homework during the lab.
2. Assign Parts 4 and 5 of the Home Practice.

Assessment

1. Use *Jocelyn's Wildflowers* Assessment Page in the *Unit Resource Guide* as a quiz.
2. Evaluate students' labs based on suggestions in the Assessment section of the Lesson Guide and in the Assessment section in the *Teacher Implementation Guide*.
3. Students save their labs in their collection folders.

Curriculum Sequence

Before This Unit

Assessment Labs, Lessons, and Portfolios

In Grades 1–4, two or three labs each year are designated assessment labs. In fourth grade, an assessment lab is in Unit 2 at the beginning of the year. This lab provides baseline information on students' abilities to collect, organize, graph, and analyze data in a lab that takes several days to complete. In Unit 8 (at midyear) and in Unit 16 (at the end of the school year), assessment labs are also included to document growth over time in these areas. Also in fourth grade, Units 2, 8, and 16 have assessment lessons that challenge students to solve open-ended problems and communicate their solutions and problem-solving strategies. Student work on these and other activities and labs are added to students' portfolios to provide a more complete progress record during the year.

Student Rubrics

In Grades 3 and 4, the three Student Rubrics *Knowing, Telling,* and *Solving* provided students with goals as they solved problems, communicated their solutions, and revised their work. In fourth grade, the three rubrics were reviewed gradually during the first semester in Units 2, 5, and 6.

Fractions and Probability

In Unit 12 of fourth grade, students explored fractions using both manipulatives and symbols. In Unit 14 they studied the probabilities involved in rolling number cubes and spinning spinners. They learned to write probabilities as fractions.

After This Unit

Assessment Labs, Lessons, and Portfolios

In fifth grade, students solve an open-ended problem *Stack Up* in Unit 2 Lesson 9, to provide more baseline data on students' current mathematical capabilities. Students add their work on this problem to their collection folders. In Unit 2 Lesson 10 *Portfolios,* they start portfolios by choosing items and making a table of contents. Student work on the baseline assessments in their portfolios will be compared to similar assessment labs and open-ended problems in Unit 8 at midyear and in Unit 16 at year's end.

Student Rubrics

In Unit 2, students use the Student Rubrics *Telling* and *Solving* as they work on the problem in Lesson 9 *Stack Up.* They continue to use the rubrics throughout the year. See the Assessment section of the *Teacher Implementation Guide* for more information on gathering baseline assessment data, assessment labs, open-ended problems, and student rubrics.

Fractions and Probability

In fifth grade, students will continue their study of probability in Unit 7. They review using fractions to express probabilities and learn to use percents. Other fraction concepts and procedures are studied in Units 3, 5, 11, 12, and 13.

Materials List

Supplies and Copies

Student	Teacher
Supplies for Each Student Group	**Supplies**
• colored square-inch tiles, at least 50 in at least 2 colors; more tiles in up to 5 colors is better (other colored items may be substituted for the tiles, e.g., links, connecting cubes, colored breakfast cereal or candy) • brown lunch bag or other opaque sack • letter-size envelope	
Copies	**Copies/Transparencies**
• 1 copy of *Jocelyn's Wildflowers* per student (*Unit Resource Guide* Page 112) • 3 copies of *Centimeter Graph Paper* per student (*Unit Resource Guide* Page 70) • 1 copy of *Three-trial Data Table* per student (*Unit Resource Guide* Page 113) • 1 copy of *Three-column Data Table* per student (*Unit Resource Guide* Page 71) • 1 copy of *Two-column Data Table* per student (*Unit Resource Guide* Page 43)	• 1 transparency of *Centimeter Graph Paper,* optional (*Unit Resource Guide* Page 70) • 1 transparency or poster of Student Rubric: *Knowing,* optional (*Teacher Implementation Guide,* Assessment section)

All blackline masters including assessment, transparency, and DPP masters are also on the Teacher Resource CD.

Student Books
Searching the Forest (*Student Guide* Pages 17–23)
Student Rubric: *Knowing* (*Student Guide* Appendix A and Inside Back Cover)

Daily Practice and Problems and Home Practice
DPP items K–P (*Unit Resource Guide* Pages 23–26)
Home Practice Parts 4–5 (*Discovery Assignment Book* Page 5)

Note: Classrooms whose pacing differs significantly from the suggested pacing of the units should use the Math Facts Calendar in Section 4 of the *Facts Resource Guide* to ensure students receive the complete math facts program.

Assessment Tools
Observational Assessment Record (*Unit Resource Guide* Pages 13–14)
Individual Assessment Record Sheet (*Teacher Implementation Guide,* Assessment section)

Daily Practice and Problems

Suggestions for using the DPPs are on page 106.

K. Bit: Subtraction Review 1 (URG p. 23)

Solve the following using paper and pencil only.

A.	1462 − 750	B.	1030 − 810	C.	1176 − 842
D.	1096 − 435	E.	1067 − 532	F.	1192 − 962
G.	1255 − 741	H.	1685 − 941	I.	1234 − 632
J.	1715 − 902	K.	1483 − 851	L.	1597 − 975

L. Task: Mental Powers (URG p. 23)

Do the following problems in your head. Be ready to share your strategies with the class.

A. $13 + 27 =$ B. $26 + 14 =$
C. $40 − 15 =$ D. $50 − 26 =$
E. $100 − 27 =$ F. $88 − 58 =$
G. $62 + 66 =$ H. $99 − 25 =$
I. $250 + 625 =$ J. $849 − 550 =$
K. $321 + 421 =$ L. $2378 + 6322 =$
M. $1000 − 478 =$ N. $8910 + 8090 =$

M. Bit: Medians (URG p. 24)

Lin, Irma, Jackie, Arti, and Jessie sold cookies for their girls' club. The following data shows the number of boxes each girl sold.

Student	Number of Boxes Sold
Lin	154 boxes
Irma	78 boxes
Arti	110 boxes
Jackie	100 boxes
Jessie	45 boxes

1. What is the median number of boxes sold?
2. How many more boxes did Lin sell than Jessie?
3. Did Irma and Jessie together sell more or less than Arti?
4. About how many boxes did the five girls sell altogether?

N. Task: Play *Digits Game* (URG p. 25)

Draw boxes like these on your paper.

□ □
+ □ □
‾‾‾‾‾‾

Your teacher or classmate will choose one card at a time from a set of cards with the digits 0–9. The cards will not be returned to the deck. As the digits are chosen, place them in the boxes. Try to find the largest sum. Remember that each digit will be read only once. Once you place a digit, it cannot be moved.

O. Bit: Subtraction Review 2 (URG p. 25)

Solve the following using paper and pencil.

A.	1079 − 772	B.	1353 − 852	C.	1669 − 845
D.	1397 − 901	E.	1265 − 963	F.	1478 − 936
G.	1887 − 926	H.	1291 − 881	I.	1198 − 943
J.	1548 − 837	K.	1379 − 657	L.	1184 − 784

P. Task: Play *Digits Game* Again (URG p. 26)

Draw boxes like these on your paper.

□ □ □
− □ □
‾‾‾‾‾‾

Your teacher or classmate will choose four digits, one at a time, from a set of cards. As each digit is read, place it in one of the boxes. Try to find the largest difference. Remember each digit will be read only once. Once you place a digit, it cannot be moved.

Searching the Forest

Populating the Forest
You are going to "populate a forest" for another group. This means you are going to put a mixture of colored tiles into a bag for another group to study.

- Agree with your group on a "recipe" for your bag. Your recipe must follow these three rules:

  A. There must be exactly 50 tiles in the bag.

  B. The number of tiles of each color must be a multiple of 10.

  C. There must be at least two different colors in the bag.

- Write down your recipe. Use a table like this one:

C Color	N Number

- Every person in your group must sign the paper with the recipe. This will show that everyone agrees that the recipe is correct.
- Count out the proper number of tiles of each color, and put the tiles in the bag. Label the bag with the initials of the people in your group.
- Seal your recipe in an envelope. Write your initials on the envelope.
- Give your envelope and the bag of tiles to your teacher.

This recipe needs a dash of blue.

Searching the Forest   SG • Grade 5 • Unit 1 • Lesson 5   **17**

Student Guide - page 17 *(Answers on p. 114)*

Experiment: Searching the Forest
You should have a bag that another group has "populated" with colored tiles. Your job is to predict the number of each color in the bag. But you cannot dump all the tiles out and count them! You are like a scientist exploring a big, deep forest. You can only look at a little bit of the forest at a time.

You are only allowed to take samples of the tiles. Each sample must have exactly ten tiles in it. After each sample, return the tiles to the bag and shake it up before you take the next sample.

Do you think we'll capture any of those rare Pink Inch Squares?

 **Draw**

1. Draw a picture of the experiment. Label the variables in your picture.
2. **A.** What are the two main variables in your experiment?
   B. Tell whether each of the main variables is categorical or numerical.
3. Why is it a good idea to shake up the bag before taking each sample?

18 SG • Grade 5 • Unit 1 • Lesson 5   Searching the Forest

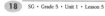

Student Guide - page 18 *(Answers on p. 114)*

Before the Lab
The Adventure Book, *A Matter of Survival,* in Lesson 4 sets the stage for this lab.

Teaching the Lab

Part 1 **Talking about Populations and Sampling**
This lab involves learning about a population by sampling. Begin by discussing situations where sampling is useful. Estimating wildlife populations, as in *A Matter of Survival,* is an important application of sampling. Similarly, the distribution of eyelets on the shoes of all the students in a school can be estimated by counting eyelets in one class and then scaling up to the number of classes in the school. This lab will help students understand how to use sampling to draw conclusions about a population, even when one cannot directly study the entire population.

Part 2 **Populating the Forest**
Students work in groups to create "populations" for other groups to study. They put colored tiles into paper bags according to certain rules. We call this "populating the forest" to underline the parallels between a rain forest and the bags: just as a rain forest might have toucans, jaguars, howler monkeys, and so on, so the bags might have red tiles, green tiles, blue tiles, and so on.

The Populating the Forest section on the *Searching the Forest* Lab Pages in the *Student Guide* is provided to help structure this activity. There are three rules for filling the bags:

1. There must be 50 tiles in each bag;
2. The number of each color must be a multiple of 10; and
3. There must be at least two different colors in the bag. Students in each group agree on a "recipe" for their bag, populate and label the bag, and seal the recipe in a labeled envelope. Every student in a group must indicate agreement with the recipe by signing it.

Have groups give you their recipes and bags for redistribution to other groups. Each group will investigate a bag populated by another group. At the end of the investigation, students predict the number of each color in their bags and compare their predictions to what is actually in the bag.

Part 3 **Identifying Variables and Drawing a Picture**
Once the "forests" are populated, the investigation begins.

Students will pull samples of ten tiles from a bag and use their data to make predictions about the populations of tiles in the bag. The Experiment: Searching the Forest section in the *Student Guide* leads students through the four phases of the TIMS Laboratory Method for this lab.

The first step is to draw a picture that indicates the procedure and identifies the key variables: Color (*C*), and the Number Pulled (*N*) *(Questions 1–2)*. Figure 12 shows a sample picture. Discuss what makes a good picture: communicating the procedure, showing the equipment, identifying the variables, and establishing notation.

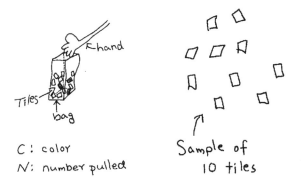

Figure 12: *Sample picture*

Part 4 **Collecting and Organizing the Data**
The next step is to gather the data. Students take three samples with ten tiles in each sample. Each time, they sort the tiles by color and record the number of each color. After each sample, all tiles should be returned to the bag and mixed thoroughly. This will ensure that the sampling is "fair" and that conclusions about the contents of the bag are unbiased *(Questions 3–4).*

After students finish the sampling, they find the median number of tiles pulled for each color in *Question 5.* (For further information about averages, see the TIMS Tutor: *Averages in the Teacher Implementation Guide.*) Figure 13 shows typical data.

C Color	N Number Pulled			
	Sample 1	Sample 2	Sample 3	Median
Red	3	4	4	4
Green	3	2	2	2
Blue	2	1	2	2
Yellow	2	3	2	2

Figure 13: *Sample data*

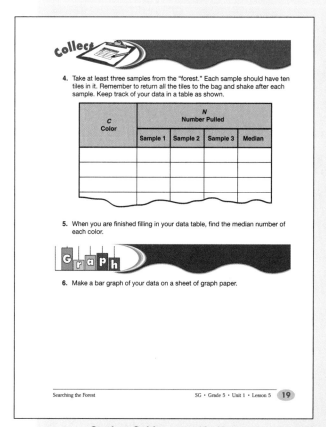

Collect

4. Take at least three samples from the "forest." Each sample should have ten tiles in it. Remember to return all the tiles to the bag and shake after each sample. Keep track of your data in a table as shown.

C Color	N Number Pulled			
	Sample 1	Sample 2	Sample 3	Median

5. When you are finished filling in your data table, find the median number of each color.

Graph

6. Make a bar graph of your data on a sheet of graph paper.

Searching the Forest   SG • Grade 5 • Unit 1 • Lesson 5 **19**

Student Guide **- page 19** *(Answers on p. 115)*

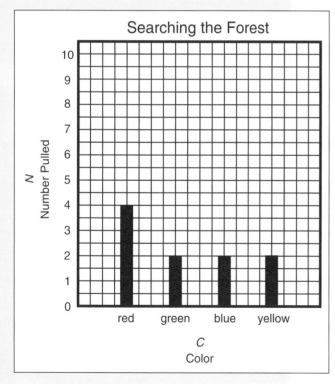

Discuss

7. **A.** What color (or colors) was most common in your samples?
   B. On average, how many of the most common color did you pull? (Use the median.)

8. **A.** What color was least common in your samples?
   B. On average, how many of the least common color did you pull? (Use the median.)

9. Predict the total number of each color in the bag. Write your predictions in a table like this one. (Remember that there are 50 tiles in all and the number of each color must be a multiple of 10.)

Color	Prediction	Actual

10. After you have made your predictions, count the number of each color that are actually in the bag. Write the actual number of each color in your table. Also, check the recipe in the envelope for your bag.

11. Did you make good predictions? Explain what happened.

Student Guide - page 20 *(Answers on p. 115)*

Searching the Forest

Figure 14: *Sample graph based on the data in Figure 13*

Part 5   Graphing the Data

In *Question 6,* students make a bar graph of the data. They graph color (*C*) on the horizontal axis and number pulled (*N*) on the vertical axis as shown in Figure 14. The median number of tiles pulled determines the height of the bars.

Part 6   Analyzing the Data

The last phase of the TIMS Laboratory Method is the analysis of the entire situation. We guide students through the analysis by posing a series of questions.

Questions 7–8 require literal comprehension of the data. Answers are found simply by examining the data table or the graph. Since answers can be found in more than one way, these questions allow you to emphasize that there are usually many ways to solve a problem, although all correct solution methods should yield the same answer. You might contrast this agreement with the case of answers based on different data: Student 1's answers based on her data may not agree with Student 2's answers based on his data, but both students might still be correct.

Questions 9–11 are the heart of the lab. Students use the data they collect to predict the number of tiles of each color in their bags. A concrete approach is to use actual tiles to make five copies of the median sample. This will usually yield 50 tiles, thus satisfying one constraint on the tile population in the bag. Next, the requirement that the number of each color be a multiple of 10 can be met by trading tiles of one color for tiles of another. The resulting set of tiles is the prediction for the contents of the bag. A more abstract way to solve the problem is to multiply the medians by five. After students record their predictions, they open the bag and count the tiles to check them. A table of predictions based on the data in Figures 13 and 14 is shown in Figure 15.

Color	Prediction	Actual
Red	20	20
Green	10	10
Blue	10	10
Yellow	10	10

Figure 15: *A table of correct predictions*

In certain cases, however, the reasoning required in *Question 9* can be quite involved. The problem can be especially hard if the total of the medians is not

10 or if some medians are odd. For example, consider the data in Figure 16.

The median sample there is two red, four green, and six blue tiles. In this case, the sum of the medians is 12, so that multiplying by five yields 60 tiles—but there are only 50 tiles in the bag, so this simple method fails. One way to solve the problem is to think it through logically. Since there are so many blue tiles in the median sample, we can assume there are at least 20 blues in the bag. There could also be 30 blues in the bag, but 40 would be too many, since there are two other colors in the bag.

So there are two cases to consider: 20 blues in the bag and 30 blues in the bag. *Case 1:* If there are 20 blues, then the other 30 tiles must be shared by red and green. Based on the medians for these colors (2 red and 4 green), 10 red and 20 green is more reasonable than 20 red and 10 green. In this case, the best prediction for the contents is 10 red, 20 green, and 20 blue. *Case 2:* If there were 30 blue tiles in the bag, then there would have to be 10 each of red and green, since both red and green appear in the samples. The prediction for the contents of the bag in this case is 10 red, 10 green, and 30 blue.

Similar reasoning is required if some of the medians are odd, since multiplying odd numbers by 5 yields numbers that are not multiples of 10. But this contradicts the requirement that the number of each color tile in the bag be a multiple of 10. So, in these cases also, students will need to use mathematical reasoning to make their predictions. In these less straightforward situations, allowing students to make more than one prediction is advisable, as long as reasons are given for each prediction.

Questions 12–15 review fractions and probability using the context of the lab. If students have not had much experience with either fractions or probability, omit these problems. Students will have many opportunities to apply fractions and probability concepts in later units.

Journal Prompt

Choose one of the following:
Write a letter to a student at another school who is having trouble solving **Question 9.** The letter can discuss how hard the problem is and should give suggestions for solving it.

Write a letter to your parents explaining what you did in this lab, what you learned, and how you might use what you learned. Give one reason you liked working in your group. Also explain one problem you had in your group and how you solved it.

C Color	N Number Pulled			
	Sample 1	Sample 2	Sample 3	Median
Red	0	4	2	2
Green	4	4	1	4
Blue	6	2	7	6

Figure 16: *A second set of data*

TIMS Tip

Questions 9–15 require deeper levels of thinking from students. Let students work on these questions unassisted for some time. Then if there are many students who cannot proceed, have a class discussion about various strategies that might work. After the discussion, students should tackle the problem again. A key notion here is that some problems cannot be solved immediately, but may require extended effort.

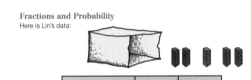

Fractions and Probability
Here is Lin's data:

Color	Prediction	Actual
Red	20	20
Green	10	10
Blue	20	20

12. A. What fraction of Lin's tiles are red?
   B. What fraction are green?
   C. What fraction are blue?

13. If Lin puts all her tiles back in the bag, mixes them up, and then picks one tile from her bag, what color or colors will she most likely pick?

Since 20 out of the 50 tiles are red, there are 20 chances out of 50 that she will pick a red tile. If Lin picks one tile out of the bag, the **probability** that she will pick a red tile is $\frac{20}{50}$.

14. A. What is the probability that Lin will pick a green tile?
   B. What is the probability that she will pick a blue tile?

15. Suppose you return all your tiles to your bag, mix them up, and pick one tile:
   A. What is the most likely color you will choose? (Note: There may be more than one.)
   B. What is the probability that you will pick that color? Write the probability as a fraction.
   C. What is the least likely color?
   D. What is the probability that you will pick that color?

Searching the Forest   SG • Grade 5 • Unit 1 • Lesson 5   **21**

Student Guide* - page 21 *(Answers on p. 116)

Student Guide - page 22

Homework

Radio Favorites

Michael asked some fifth-grade students at his school about the type of music played on their favorite radio stations. This is what he found:

Type of Music	Number of Students
classical	2
alternative rock	4
oldies	4
country and western	6
rock	5
rap	4

1. How many students did Michael survey?

2. **A.** Is Type of Music a numerical or categorical variable? How can you tell?
   B. Is Number of Students a numerical or categorical variable? How can you tell?

3. What was the most popular type of music?

4. You may want to organize your answers to this question in a table.
   A. What fraction of the sample liked each type of music?
   B. There are 100 fifth-grade students altogether in Michael's school. Estimate how many fifth graders like each type of music.

5. Describe a survey you would like to carry out. Tell what variables you would study and what values of those variables you would expect. (For example, the variables Michael studied were type of music and the number of students. The values of type of music were classical, alternative rock, oldies, etc.)

Student Guide - page 22 (Answers on p. 116)

Student Guide - page 23

Candy Grab

You will need a sheet of graph paper to complete this part of the homework.

Alexis pulled candies from a brown bag. This is her data:

C Color	N Number Pulled			
	Sample 1	Sample 2	Sample 3	Median
red	6	8	5	
green	2	1	2	
blue	2	1	3	

6. What is the median number for each color?

7. Make a bar graph of Alexis's data.

8. If Alexis takes another sample, which color would be most common? Why do you think so?

9. Alexis's bag has 50 candies. The number of each color is a multiple of 10. How many candies of each color do you think are in the bag?

Use your answer to Question 9 to answer Question 10.

10. Suppose Alexis pulls just one candy from the bag.
    A. What is the probability that the candy is red?
    B. What is the probability that the candy is green?
    C. What is the probability that the candy is blue?

Student Guide - page 23 (Answers on p. 117)

Math Facts

Daily Practice and Problems items K and O provide an opportunity to identify any students who do not yet have fluency with the subtraction facts. For those students who need extra practice with these facts, use the Addition and Subtraction Math Facts Review section in the *Facts Resource Guide* for fifth grade.

Homework and Practice

- Assign the Candy Grab and Radio Favorites sections of the *Searching the Forest* Lab Pages for homework during the lab. The data analysis required is similar to that in the lab. Students will need graph paper for Candy Grab. If you did not assign the fractions and probability questions in the lab, do not assign **Question 10** in the Homework section.

- Assign Daily Practice and Problems item L to develop mental math strategies for addition.

- Use item M as a quick review of finding the median of a data set.

- Items N and P introduce the *Digits Game*. This game works well as a warm-up activity. It develops number sense while providing computation practice. Ask students to lead the game and choose their own configuration of the boxes.

- Assign Part 4 of the Home Practice in the *Discovery Assignment Book* for addition and subtraction practice. Assign Part 5 for practice with graphing. Students will need a piece of *Centimeter Graph Paper* for Part 5.

Answers for Parts 4 and 5 of the Home Practice are in the Answer Key at the end of this lesson and at the end of this unit.

This lab is designated a baseline assessment lab—not as a test to see if students have mastered the concepts taught in the lab, but as a record of students' abilities at this point in the school year. In this way you, as well as students and parents, will be able to see improvements in students' mathematical, organizational, and analytic skills over time. The ideas listed below can help you begin an assessment program that documents students' current skill levels and their future accomplishments. Choose the components that best fit your needs. More information on each idea that follows can be found in the Assessment section of the *Teacher Implementation Guide.*

Collection Folders and Portfolios. Begin a collection folder for each student. These will be used throughout the year to save samples of students' work that is appropriate for inclusion in a portfolio. Ask students to write their names on a folder, place their completed labs in their collection folders, and file them in a central location in the room. As the year progresses, you may designate specific activities that students should save in their collection folders. If students are proud of particular items, then they may add these to their collection folders as well. In Unit 2 Lesson 10 *Portfolios,* students choose items from their collection folders to begin their portfolios, which will eventually include a record of their work throughout the year. See the TIMS Tutor: *Portfolios* in the *Teacher Implementation Guide* for more information on using portfolios.

Observational Assessment Record. Observe students as they work in groups through each of the steps in the TIMS Laboratory Method. Record your observations on the *Observational Assessment Record* found at the beginning of the *Unit Resource Guide* for this unit and on students' *Individual Assessment Record Sheets.* The *Individual Assessment Record Sheets* are in the Assessment section in the *Teacher Implementation Guide* and can be stored in students' portfolios. Since it is not practical to make and record observations on all the students in a class during one activity, choose a small group of students to observe during this lab. Then, during subsequent labs, observe different groups of students.

Name _____ Date _____

PART 4 **Addition and Subtraction Practice**

Solve the following problems using paper and pencil only. Estimate to make sure your answers are reasonable.

A. 75 + 39 =   B. 167 + 74 =   C. 254 − 118 =

D. 7046 + 856 =   E. 9233 − 560 =   F. 8570 + 2545 =

G. 5649 − 1850 =   H. 5503 + 7098 =   I. 6800 − 4874 =

PART 5 **Number of Windows**

Brandon collected data on the number of windows in each room of his home. His data is shown below. Make a bar graph of Brandon's data on a piece of graph paper. Label the horizontal axis with the variable, Number of Windows.

Number of Windows	Number of Rooms
0	0
1	2
2	3
3	0
4	1

1. What is the most common number of windows in the rooms in Brandon's home?

2. How many windows are in Brandon's home altogether?

POPULATIONS AND SAMPLES   DAB · Grade 5 · Unit 1   **5**

Discovery Assignment Book - page 5 *(Answers on p. 117)*

Student Rubric: Knowing

What is a rubric?

It tells me how to make sure I've done my best work!

In My Best Work in Mathematics:

- I show that I understand the ideas in the problem.

- I show the same mathematical ideas in different ways. I use pictures, tables, graphs, and sentences when they fit the problem.

- I show that I can use tools and rules correctly.

- I show that I can use the mathematical facts that apply to the problem.

SG • Grade 5 • Appendix A **501**

Student Guide **- Appendix A**

Student Rubrics. The student rubrics communicate to students what we value in mathematics and criteria for excellence. A copy of the Student Rubric: *Knowing* can be found in Appendix A of the *Student Guide* or on the inside back cover of the *Student Guide.* Review the rubric with students so they can use it as a guide as they complete the lab. You can also make a poster or transparency of the rubric using the blackline masters in the Assessment section of the *Teacher Implementation Guide.* (Students will review the remaining two student rubrics in Unit 2.)

Evaluating the Lab. Teachers often use a point system to grade a lab or a portion of the lab. You may choose to grade the graph for this lab and the picture for the next. Points can be assigned based on the following criteria:

1. Drawing the Picture
   - Did students show the lab procedure: pulling a handful of tiles from the bag, sorting the tiles by color, and counting each color?
   - Did students identify the two variables as Color (C) and Number of Tiles (N)?

2. Collecting and Recording Data
   - Did students fill in the headings of the data table correctly?
   - Did students record the data correctly?
   - Did students correctly find the medians for each color of tile?

3. Graphing the Data
   - Do students' graphs have titles?
   - Are the horizontal axes labeled with the variable Color (C) and the vertical axes labeled with Number of Tiles (N)?
   - Are the vertical axes scaled appropriately?
   - Did students draw the bars on the lines labeled with the appropriate color? Are they the correct height?

4. Exploring the Data
   - Are the answers correct based on the data?
   - Did students give complete responses when asked to explain solutions?

Assessment Page. The *Jocelyn's Wildflowers* Assessment Page in the *Unit Resource Guide* presents a simple sampling problem similar to the situation in *Searching the Forest* and can be used as a quiz. Students will need a piece of graph paper to complete this assessment.

Make a learning station with a 500-tile forest using the same rules from the lab. (The number of tiles of each color must be a multiple of ten and there must be at least two different colors in the bag.) Have each child take a sample of twenty tiles. (Each sample should be returned to the class grab bag before the next sample is taken.) Individual samples are recorded on a class data table. When all samples are recorded, then every student should analyze the data and predict the number of each color in the bag. You might give a prize for the best prediction.

Software Connection

Students can graph their data using *Graph Master* or a similar graphing and data analysis program. Students can enter their data in the computer using just two columns, the first column for Color and the second column for the Median Number Pulled. (They need not enter their data for each sample.) Once the data is entered, they use the graph function to make a bar graph. Students can also experiment with using other types of graphs such as circle graphs or pictographs to display their data.

At a Glance

Math Facts and Daily Practice and Problems

1. Use Bits K and O to assess students' fluency with the subtraction facts.
2. Use Bit M for practice finding medians and Tasks L, N, and P to develop number sense and provide computation practice.

Part 1. Talking about Populations and Sampling

Discuss populations and sampling relating them to students' previous experiences, including the Adventure Book *A Matter of Survival* and the lab *Eyelets*.

Part 2. Populating the Forest

1. Using the *Searching the Forest* Lab Pages as a guide, student groups make "recipes" for putting colored square-inch tiles in lunch bags. Each bag must have exactly 50 tiles of at least two colors, and the number of tiles of each color must be a multiple of ten.
2. Students fill bags according to their recipes and initial the bags.
3. Students sign their recipes and seal them in an envelope, also labeled with their initials.
4. Students turn in bags and recipes to the teacher, who redistributes them to other groups.

Part 3. Identifying Variables and Drawing a Picture

1. Review the Student Rubric: *Knowing* in the *Student Guide*. Encourage students to use the rubric as a guide as they work on the lab.
2. Following the *Searching the Forest* Lab Pages, students draw a picture showing the main variables in the experiment (Color and Number) and indicating the procedure. *(Questions 1–2)*

Part 4. Collecting and Organizing the Data

Students pull three samples of ten tiles each from "forests" populated by other students. They record the data in a table and find the median for each color. *(Questions 3–5)*

Part 5. Graphing the Data

Students make bar graphs of their data. *(Question 6)*

Part 6. Analyzing the Data

1. Students answer questions about the lab and predict the contents of the bag. Then they open the bags and check their predictions. *(Questions 7–11)*
2. *Questions 12–15* review fractions and probability using the lab data. If students are unfamiliar with either of these topics, omit these questions.

Homework

1. You can use Radio Favorites and Candy Grab in the Homework section of the *Student Guide* for homework during the lab.
2. Assign Parts 4 and 5 of the Home Practice.

At a Glance

Assessment

1. Use *Jocelyn's Wildflowers* Assessment Page in the *Unit Resource Guide* as a quiz.
2. Evaluate students' labs based on the suggestions in the Assessment section of the Lesson Guide and in the Assessment section in the *Teacher Implementation Guide*.
3. Students save their labs in their collection folders.

Extension

Make a learning station with a 500-tile forest using the same rules from the lab. Have each student take a sample of 20 tiles and record their data on a class table. When all samples are recorded, have students predict the number of each color in the bag.

Connection

Have students graph their data using a program such as *Graph Master*.

Answer Key is on pages 114–118.

Notes:

Name _____ Date _____

Jocelyn's Wildflowers

Jocelyn volunteers at the County Road Prairie for the Prairie Restoration Project. Her assignment is counting certain types of wildflowers in several equal-sized areas. Her data are shown below.

T Type of Wildflower	N Number Jocelyn Counted			
	Area 1	Area 2	Area 3	Median
Prairie Dock	8	6	8	
Black-eyed Susan	5	6	6	
Purple Cone Flower	3	4	5	
Goldenrod	10	9	12	

1. In the table above, fill in the median number of wildflowers Jocelyn counted.

2. Make a bar graph of Jocelyn's data.

3. The entire County Road Prairie is 50 times the size of one of the areas that Jocelyn counted. Estimate the number of each type of wildflower in the entire County Road Prairie. Explain how you made your estimate.

Type of Wildflower	Estimated Number in County Road Prairie
Prairie Dock	
Black-eyed Susan	
Purple Cone Flower	
Goldenrod	

Assessment Blackline Master

_____

	Trial 1	Trial 2	Trial 3	Average

Searching the Forest

Populating the Forest

You are going to "populate a forest" for another group. This means you are going to put a mixture of colored tiles into a bag for another group to study.

- Agree with your group on a "recipe" for your bag. Your recipe must follow these three rules:
  A. There must be exactly 50 tiles in the bag.
  B. The number of tiles of each color must be a multiple of 10.
  C. There must be at least two different colors in the bag.
- Write down your recipe. Use a table like this one:

C Color	N Number

- Every person in your group must sign the paper with the recipe. This will show that everyone agrees that the recipe is correct.
- Count out the proper number of tiles of each color, and put the tiles in the bag. Label the bag with the initials of the people in your group.
- Seal your recipe in an envelope. Write your initials on the envelope.
- Give your envelope and the bag of tiles to your teacher.

This recipe needs a dash of blue.

Searching the Forest   SG • Grade 5 • Unit 1 • Lesson 5   **17**

Student Guide - page 17

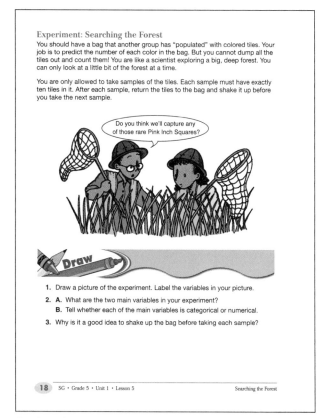

Experiment: Searching the Forest

You should have a bag that another group has "populated" with colored tiles. Your job is to predict the number of each color in the bag. But you cannot dump all the tiles out and count them! You are like a scientist exploring a big, deep forest. You can only look at a little bit of the forest at a time.

You are only allowed to take samples of the tiles. Each sample must have exactly ten tiles in it. After each sample, return the tiles to the bag and shake it up before you take the next sample.

Do you think we'll capture any of those rare Pink Inch Squares?

Draw

1. Draw a picture of the experiment. Label the variables in your picture.
2. **A.** What are the two main variables in your experiment?
   B. Tell whether each of the main variables is categorical or numerical.
3. Why is it a good idea to shake up the bag before taking each sample?

18   SG • Grade 5 • Unit 1 • Lesson 5   Searching the Forest

Student Guide - page 18

Student Guide (pp. 17–18)

1. See sample picture in Figure 12 in Lesson Guide 5.*

2. **A.** Color and number pulled*

   B. Color is categorical and number pulled is numerical.

3. The person who pulls the next sample does not pull the same tiles as the person who pulled the previous sample.*

*Answers and/or discussion are included in the Lesson Guide.

Student Guide (p. 19)

4. See sample data table in Figure 13 in Lesson Guide 5.*

5. See sample data table in Figure 13 in Lesson Guide 5.*

6. See the sample graph in Figure 14 in Lesson Guide 5.*

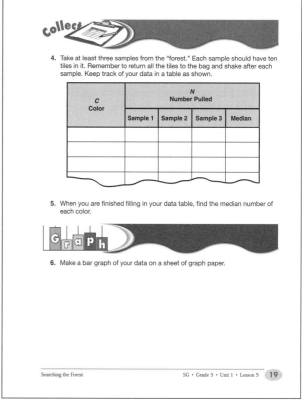

Student Guide - page 19

Student Guide (p. 20)

The answers to *Questions 7–11* are based on the sample data in Figures 13–14 in Lesson Guide 5.

7. A. Answers will vary. Using sample data: red.

  B. Answers will vary. Using sample data: 4.

8. A. Answers will vary. Using sample data: green, blue, yellow.

  B. Answers will vary. Using sample data: 2, 2, 2.

9.–10. See sample table in Figure 15 in Lesson Guide 5.*

11. Answers will vary.*

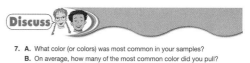
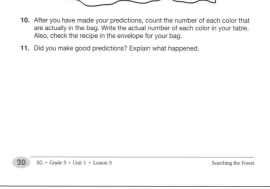

Student Guide - page 20

*Answers and/or discussion are included in the Lesson Guide.

Fractions and Probability
Here is Lin's data:

Color	Prediction	Actual
Red	20	20
Green	10	10
Blue	20	20

12. **A.** What fraction of Lin's tiles are red?
B. What fraction are green?
C. What fraction are blue?

13. If Lin puts all her tiles back in the bag, mixes them up, and then picks one tile from her bag, what color or colors will she most likely pick?

Since 20 out of the 50 tiles are red, there are 20 chances out of 50 that she will pick a red tile. If Lin picks one tile out of the bag, the **probability** that she will pick a red tile is $\frac{20}{50}$.

14. **A.** What is the probability that Lin will pick a green tile?
B. What is the probability that she will pick a blue tile?

15. Suppose you return all your tiles to your bag, mix them up, and pick one tile:
A. What is the most likely color you will choose? (Note: There may be more than one.)
B. What is the probability that you will pick that color? Write the probability as a fraction.
C. What is the least likely color?
D. What is the probability that you will pick that color?

Searching the Forest   SG • Grade 5 • Unit 1 • Lesson 5   **21**

Student Guide - page 21

Radio Favorites
Michael asked some fifth-grade students at his school about the type of music played on their favorite radio stations. This is what he found:

Type of Music	Number of Students
classical	2
alternative rock	4
oldies	4
country and western	6
rock	5
rap	4

1. How many students did Michael survey?
2. **A.** Is Type of Music a numerical or categorical variable? How can you tell?
B. Is Number of Students a numerical or categorical variable? How can you tell?
3. What was the most popular type of music?
4. You may want to organize your answers to this question in a table.
A. What fraction of the sample liked each type of music?
B. There are 100 fifth-grade students altogether in Michael's school. Estimate how many fifth graders like each type of music.
5. Describe a survey you would like to carry out. Tell what variables you would study and what values of those variables you would expect. (For example, the variables Michael studied were type of music and the number of students. The values of type of music were classical, alternative rock, oldies, etc.)

22 SG • Grade 5 • Unit 1 • Lesson 5   Searching the Forest

Student Guide - page 22

Student Guide (p. 21)

12. A. $\frac{20}{50}$ **B.** $\frac{10}{50}$ **C.** $\frac{20}{50}$

13. blue or red

14. A. $\frac{10}{50}$ **B.** $\frac{20}{50}$

15. A. Answers will vary. Using sample data: red.
B. $\frac{20}{50}$
C. Answers will vary. Using sample data: green, blue, yellow.
D. Answers will vary. Using sample data: $\frac{10}{50}, \frac{10}{50}, \frac{10}{50}$.

Student Guide (p. 22)

Homework

1. 25 students
2. A. categorical
B. numerical
3. country and western
4. A.

Type of Music	Fractions	Number of Students
classical	$\frac{2}{25}$	8
alternative rock	$\frac{4}{25}$	16
oldies	$\frac{4}{25}$	16
country and western	$\frac{6}{25}$	24
rock	$\frac{5}{25}$	20
rap	$\frac{4}{25}$	16

B. Answers will vary. Multiplying each number in the sample by 4: classical is 8 students, alternative rock is 16 students, oldies is 16 students, country and western is 24 students, rock is 20 students, rap is 16 students.

5. Answers will vary.

Student Guide (p. 23)

6. red is 6, green is 2, blue is 2

7.

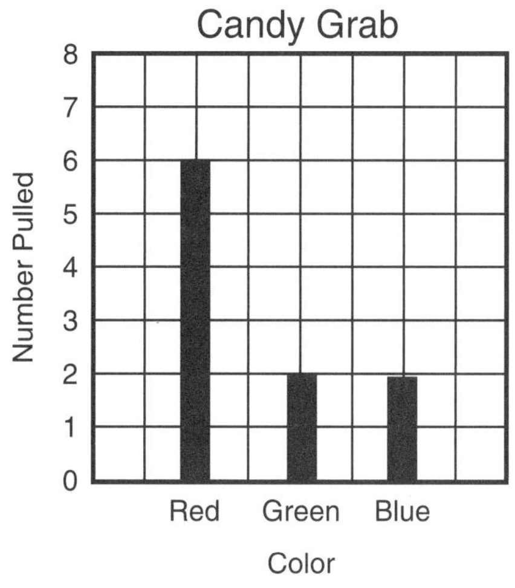

Candy Grab

(bar graph: vertical axis "Number Pulled" labeled 0–8, horizontal axis "Color" with Red = 6, Green = 2, Blue = 2)

8. Red is the most likely color because it had the highest median for the first three samples.

9. Based on the data: 30 red, 10 green, 10 blue.

10. A. $\frac{30}{50}$ **B.** $\frac{10}{50}$ **C.** $\frac{10}{50}$

Candy Grab

You will need a sheet of graph paper to complete this part of the homework.

Alexis pulled candies from a brown bag. This is her data:

C Color	N Number Pulled			
	Sample 1	Sample 2	Sample 3	Median
red	6	8	5	
green	2	1	2	
blue	2	1	3	

6. What is the median number for each color?

7. Make a bar graph of Alexis's data.

8. If Alexis takes another sample, which color would be most common? Why do you think so?

9. Alexis's bag has 50 candies. The number of each color is a multiple of 10. How many candies of each color do you think are in the bag?

Use your answer to Question 9 to answer Question 10.

10. Suppose Alexis pulls just one candy from the bag.
   A. What is the probability that the candy is red?
   B. What is the probability that the candy is green?
   C. What is the probability that the candy is blue?

Student Guide - page 23

Discovery Assignment Book (p. 5)

Home Practice*

Part 4. Addition and Subtraction Practice

A. 114   **B.** 241   **C.** 136

D. 7902   **E.** 8673   **F.** 11,115

G. 3799   **H.** 12,601   **I.** 1926

Part 5. Number of Windows

Windows in Brandon's House

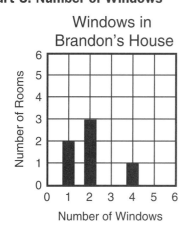

I. 2 windows

2. 12 windows

Name _____ Date _____

PART 4 **Addition and Subtraction Practice**
Solve the following problems using paper and pencil only. Estimate to make sure your answers are reasonable.

A. 75 + 39 =   B. 167 + 74 =   C. 254 − 118 =

D. 7046 + 856 =   E. 9233 − 560 =   F. 8570 + 2545 =

G. 5649 − 1850 =   H. 5503 + 7098 =   I. 6800 − 4874 =

PART 5 **Number of Windows**
Brandon collected data on the number of windows in each room of his home. His data is shown below. Make a bar graph of Brandon's data on a piece of graph paper. Label the horizontal axis with the variable, Number of Windows.

Number of Windows	Number of Rooms
0	0
1	2
2	3
3	0
4	1

1. What is the most common number of windows in the rooms in Brandon's home?

2. How many windows are in Brandon's home altogether?

Discovery Assignment Book - page 5

*Answers for all the Home Practice in the *Discovery Assignment Book* are at the end of the unit.

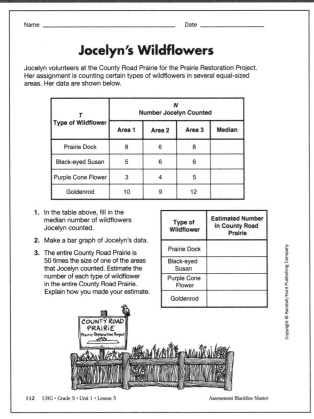

Unit Resource Guide - page 112

Unit Resource Guide (p. 112)

Jocelyn's Wildflowers

1. 8, 6, 4, 10

2.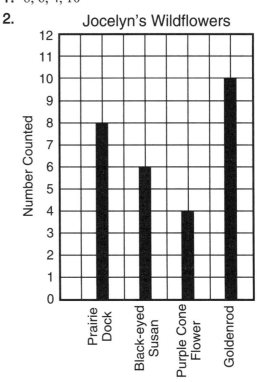

3. Estimates based on multiplying the median numbers of flowers by 50

Type of Wildflower	Estimated Number in County Road Prairie
Prairie Dock	400
Black-eyed Susan	300
Purple Cone Flower	200
Goldenrod	500

Practice Problems

Lesson Overview

Estimated Class Sessions

1

Students solve a variety of multistep word problems.

Key Content

- Solving multistep word problems.
- Communicating solutions orally and in writing.
- Choosing appropriate methods and tools (calculator, pencil and paper, or mental math) to calculate.
- Choosing to find an estimate or an exact answer.

Math Facts

Use the Addition and Subtraction Math Facts Review section of the *Facts Resource Guide* as needed.

Homework

1. Assign some or all of the problems for homework.
2. Assign Part 6 of the Home Practice.

Materials List

Supplies and Copies

Student	Teacher
Supplies for Each Student • calculator	**Supplies**
Copies	**Copies/Transparencies**

All blackline masters including assessment, transparency, and DPP masters are also on the Teacher Resource CD.

Student Books
Practice Problems (*Student Guide* Page 24)

Daily Practice and Problems and Home Practice
DPP items Q–R (*Unit Resource Guide* Pages 26–27)
Home Practice Part 6 (*Discovery Assignment Book* Page 6)

Note: Classrooms whose pacing differs significantly from the suggested pacing of the units should use the Math Facts Calendar in Section 4 of the *Facts Resource Guide* to ensure students receive the complete math facts program.

Daily Practice and Problems

Suggestions for using the DPPs are on page 122.

Q. Bit: Median Height (URG p. 26)

1. Find the median height of the Presidents listed below.
2. Find the median weight of the Presidents listed below.

President	Height	Weight
Dwight Eisenhower	5 ft 10 in	180 lbs
John Kennedy	6 ft	175 lbs
Lyndon Johnson	6 ft 3 in	210 lbs
Richard Nixon	5 ft 11 in	175 lbs
Gerald Ford	6 ft	200 lbs
Jimmy Carter	5 ft 9 in	175 lbs
Ronald Reagan	6 ft 1in	185 lbs
George H. W. Bush	6 ft 2 in	195 lbs

R. Task: Addition and Subtraction
(URG p. 27)

Solve the following in your head or using paper and pencil. Estimate to make sure your answers are reasonable.

A. $65 + 79 =$

B. $460 - 183 =$

C. $783 - 594 =$

D. $1089 - 437 =$

E. $2378 + 587 =$

F. $9045 + 2985 =$

Many activities and labs in *Math Trailblazers* have word problems for students to solve. In most units, however, we provide an additional set of word problems that may not be linked to any specific activity or lab. This lesson guide is a brief introduction to these problem sets. For further information, see the TIMS Tutor: *Word Problems* in the *Teacher Implementation Guide.*

These problem sets serve several purposes. They present opportunities to practice choosing appropriate methods to solve problems. Common and useful strategies include table building, guessing and checking, drawing pictures, looking for an easier related problem, estimating, and working backwards. Students may choose to use paper and pencil, mental math, or calculators to compute. For some problems, an exact answer is necessary. For others, an estimate is appropriate. Use these problem sets to focus on strategies from time to time.

The sets intentionally include a wide variety of problems. We want students to think through each problem individually rather than simply to apply the same procedure to several problems in a row. Students then may choose the appropriate tool or strategy to solve each problem.

Using the Problems. Students can use the problems in several ways. They can work on them individually, in pairs, or in groups. One approach is to ask students to work on the problems individually at first, and then to compare solutions in pairs or small groups. Then, the small-group solutions can be shared with other groups in a class discussion. You can also assign the problems for homework. And, because this activity does not require much teacher preparation, it is appropriate to leave for a substitute teacher.

Discussing Solutions. Students learn a great deal about the problem-solving process and mathematics when solutions are explained, compared, and contrasted. Therefore, it is important that students discuss the problems they solve. Such discussions remind children that there are usually several ways to solve a problem and that while accuracy is important, communicating a solution path is also important. From listening to others, they may hear that although a problem is difficult, sticking with it by trying different strategies is worthwhile. These are high expectations for students. At the beginning

Practice Problems

Choose an appropriate method to solve each of the following problems. For some questions you may need to find an exact answer. For others you may only need an estimate. Use appropriate tools such as calculators, paper and pencil, mental math, or estimation.

1. A company has 1000 jump ropes that need to be put in packages of 5 jump ropes each. How many packages are needed?

2. Three friends want to evenly split the cost of a pizza. If the pizza costs $5, then about how much should each person pay?

3. A disc factory has 10,000 CDs to ship to stores. The factory shipped 30 boxes that hold 200 CDs each and 5 boxes that hold 100 CDs each. How many CDs are left to be shipped?

4. Five classes went to the museum. There are 24 students in each class. Two classes went on Tuesday. The remaining classes went on Wednesday.
   A. How many students went on Tuesday?
   B. How many students went on Wednesday?
   C. How many students went to the museum in all?

5. Three boxes of bananas, three boxes of oranges, and three boxes of apples were sent to a school lunchroom. All the boxes weighed the same, and altogether the fruit weighed 270 pounds. How many pounds of each kind of fruit were sent to the lunchroom?

6. In five days, a fruit stand had sales of $158, $139, $225, $195, and $125. The total expenses for the five days were $500. About how much profit did the fruit stand make? (Profit is the amount of money earned after all expenses are paid.)

7. Jerry bowled three games. His scores were 120, 87, and 123. Find his median score.

Student Guide - page 24 (Answers on p. 124)

Name _____ Date _____

PART 6 Solving Problems

Choose an appropriate method to solve each of the following problems. For some questions you may need to find an exact answer, while for others you may only need an estimate. For each question, you may choose to use paper and pencil, mental math, or a calculator. Be prepared to tell the class how you solved each problem.

1. Michael's mother baked 3 dozen cookies for Michael's birthday party. If seven friends are coming to the party, how many cookies can each child have if they share the cookies equally? (*Hint:* Don't forget to give Michael some cookies.)

2. The gym teacher bought 50 balls for the high school. He bought 35 tennis balls that cost 60¢ each. The rest of the balls were golf balls that cost $1.25 each. How much money did he spend altogether?

3. Mr. Moreno went to Springfield for a four-day weekend. He stayed at a hotel for three nights. The bill was $267. What was the rate for each night?

4. Irma is shopping with her cousin Maria, who recently got married. As a wedding gift, Maria received a $100 gift certificate at a department store. She finds the following items that she wants to buy: a comforter for $48, two pillows for $23 each, a waffle maker for $39, three picture frames for $5.95 each, and a cookbook for $12. Since she only has $100 to spend, make a list of the items she can purchase with her gift certificate. Explain your thinking.

Discovery Assignment Book - page 6 (Answers on p. 124)

---

of the year, students may struggle with the problem-solving process, but as they continue to solve problems throughout the year, they will become more confident and successful thinkers and communicators.

Problem Strategies. The *Practice Problems* Activity Page has seven problems that can be solved in a variety of ways. *Question 1* can be solved using paper and pencil, mental math, or a calculator. Students can simply divide $1000 \div 5 = 200$ packages.

Students can use estimation to solve *Question 2.* The $5 can be thought of as $6 to get an estimate of $2 each. Students should realize that each friend's share is less than $2. Students might want to find the actual solution to this problem. Since $5 cannot be divided evenly between 3 people, two of the three people will have to pay 1 more cent to actually buy the pizza.

In *Question 6,* students should choose to estimate since the question asks for an approximate answer. Students can use convenient numbers for each dollar amount given. Possible convenient numbers are: $150, $150, $225, $200, and $125. Students then must sum their convenient numbers to find the sales made. Another possible strategy is to estimate total sales by grouping pairs of numbers as shown: $158 + $139 is about $300; $225 + $125 is $350; and $195 is about $200. So, total sales are about $300 + $350 + $200 or $850. Since the sales ($850 with convenient numbers listed above) are greater than the expenses, $500, there is a profit of approximately $350.

Homework and Practice

- Assign some or all of the problems for homework.
- Use Task R from the Daily Practice and Problems for practice adding and subtracting. Ask students to describe their estimation strategies for at least one problem.
- Assign Part 6 of Home Practice in the *Discovery Assignment Book* for further practice solving word problems.

Answers for Part 6 of the Home Practice are in the Answer Key at the end of this lesson and at the end of this unit.

Math Facts and Daily Practice and Problems

Assign Bit Q and Task R from the Daily Practice and Problems.

Teaching the Activity

1. Students solve *Questions 1–7* on the *Practice Problems* Activity Page in the *Student Guide.* They can work individually or in small groups. Calculators should be available.
2. Students discuss their solution strategies with the class.

Homework

1. Assign some or all of the problems for homework.
2. Assign Part 6 of the Home Practice.

Answer Key is on page 124.

Notes:

Practice Problems

Choose an appropriate method to solve each of the following problems. For some questions you may need to find an exact answer. For others you may only need an estimate. Use appropriate tools such as calculators, paper and pencil, mental math, or estimation.

1. A company has 1000 jump ropes that need to be put in packages of 5 jump ropes each. How many packages are needed?

2. Three friends want to evenly split the cost of a pizza. If the pizza costs $5, then about how much should each person pay?

3. A disc factory has 10,000 CDs to ship to stores. The factory shipped 30 boxes that hold 200 CDs each and 5 boxes that hold 100 CDs each. How many CDs are left to be shipped?

4. Five classes went to the museum. There are 24 students in each class. Two classes went on Tuesday. The remaining classes went on Wednesday.
   A. How many students went on Tuesday?
   B. How many students went on Wednesday?
   C. How many students went to the museum in all?

5. Three boxes of bananas, three boxes of oranges, and three boxes of apples were sent to a school lunchroom. All the boxes weighed the same, and altogether the fruit weighed 270 pounds. How many pounds of each kind of fruit were sent to the lunchroom?

6. In five days, a fruit stand had sales of $158, $139, $225, $195, and $125. The total expenses for the five days were $500. About how much profit did the fruit stand make? (Profit is the amount of money earned after all expenses are paid.)

7. Jerry bowled three games. His scores were 120, 87, and 123. Find his median score.

Student Guide - page 24

Name _____ Date _____

PART 6 **Solving Problems**

Choose an appropriate method to solve each of the following problems. For some questions you may need to find an exact answer, while for others you may only need an estimate. For each question, you may choose to use paper and pencil, mental math, or a calculator. Be prepared to tell the class how you solved each problem.

1. Michael's mother baked 3 dozen cookies for Michael's birthday party. If seven friends are coming to the party, how many cookies can each child have if they share the cookies equally? (*Hint:* Don't forget to give Michael some cookies.)

2. The gym teacher bought 50 balls for the high school. He bought 35 tennis balls that cost 60¢ each. The rest of the balls were golf balls that cost $1.25 each. How much money did he spend altogether?

3. Mr. Moreno went to Springfield for a four-day weekend. He stayed at a hotel for three nights. The bill was $267. What was the rate for each night?

4. Irma is shopping with her cousin Maria, who recently got married. As a wedding gift, Maria received a $100 gift certificate at a department store. She finds the following items that she wants to buy: a comforter for $48, two pillows for $23 each, a waffle maker for $39, three picture frames for $5.95 each, and a cookbook for $12. Since she only has $100 to spend, make a list of the items she can purchase with her gift certificate. Explain your thinking.

Discovery Assignment Book - page 6

Student Guide (p. 24)

Practice Problems

1. 200 packages*

2. Estimates will vary. One possible estimate is about $1.70.*

3. 3500 CDs

4. **A.** 48 students
   B. 72 students
   C. 120 students

5. 90 pounds of each

6. Estimates will vary. Using the following convenient numbers $150 + $150 + $225 + $200 + $125, total sales were about $850. So profit was about $850 − $500 or $350.*

7. 120

Discovery Assignment Book (p. 6)

Home Practice[†]

Part 6. Solving Problems

1. 4 cookies each with 4 cookies left or $4\frac{1}{2}$ cookies each.

2. $39.75

3. $89.00

4. Answers will vary. One possible purchase is a comforter and two pillows for $94.00.

---

*Answers and/or discussion are included in the Lesson Guide.
[†]Answers for all the Home Practice in the *Discovery Assignment Book* are at the end of the unit.

Discovery Assignment Book (p. 3)

Part 1. Addition and Subtraction

A. 120	**B.** 110
C. 70	**D.** 98
E. 320	**F.** 68
G. 900	**H.** 1364
I. 400	

Part 2. Variables and Values in Your Home

I. A. Type of vegetable; categorical.

   B. Answers will vary. Four possible responses include: carrots, broccoli, celery, and cauliflower.

2. A. Time in minutes; numerical.

   B. Answers will vary. Four possible responses include: 15 minutes, 20 minutes, 1 hour, and 5 minutes.

3. A. Type of sandwich; categorical.

   B. Answers will vary. Four possible responses include: ham, turkey, tuna, and cheese.

Discovery Assignment Book (p. 4)

Part 3. Finding the Median

I. 18 videos

2. 24 eyelets

3. 5 pairs of shoes, 5 pairs of shoes

4. $1.45

5. Answers will vary. Everyone in the family can line up by height, then measure the height of the person in the middle.

Name _____ Date _____

Unit 1 **Home Practice**

PART 1 **Addition and Subtraction**
Solve the following problems in your head.

A. 30 + 90 = _____   B. 50 + 60 = _____   C. 160 − 90 = _____

D. 148 − 50 = _____   E. 240 + 80 = _____   F. 100 − 32 = _____

G. 650 + 250 = _____   H. 732 + 632 = _____   I. 389 + 11 = _____

On another sheet of paper, explain how you solved two of the problems in your head.

PART 2 **Variables and Values in Your Home**

I. A. David asks each of his family members what his or her favorite vegetable is. Is he collecting data on a numerical or categorical variable?

   B. List four possible values for this variable.

2. A. Alexis asks her classmates how long it takes them to get to school. What variable is she studying? Is it numerical or categorical?

   B. List four possible values for this variable. (*Hint:* How long does it take you to get to school? How long does it take your friends?)

3. A. Brandon asks his friends what type of sandwiches they are going to order at the fast-food restaurant. Is he collecting data on a numerical or categorical variable?

   B. List four possible values for this variable.

POPULATIONS AND SAMPLES   DAB • Grade 5 • Unit 1   **3**

Discovery Assignment Book - page 3

Name _____ Date _____

PART 3 **Finding the Median**
Find the median for each set of data given below. Show how you decided.

I. Roberto, David, Nila, Lee Yah, and Romesh compared the number of videos their families own. Roberto owns 47 videos while David only owns 4. Nila owns 23 videos, Lee Yah owns 18 videos, and Romesh owns 15 videos. What is the median number of videos? (*Hint:* First list the number of videos owned by each family in order from smallest to largest. You should list five numbers.)

2. Brandon compared five different types of basketball shoes. His favorite brand has 24 eyelets. His least favorite has 32 eyelets. Two brands have pairs of shoes with 20 eyelets. Another brand has 28 eyelets. What is the median number of eyelets? (*Hint:* List the number 20 twice since two pairs of shoes have 20 eyelets.)

3. There are seven people in Felicia's family. Four members of her family have 5 pairs of shoes. Two members of her family have 3 pairs of shoes. Her mother has 15 pairs of shoes. What is the median number of pairs of shoes in Felicia's household? What is the mode? (*Hint:* List the number 5 four times since four members have 5 pairs of shoes. List the number 3 twice.)

4. Four people in David's family celebrate birthdays in September. David buys 4 cards. The card for his mother costs $2.25. The cards for his two brothers are $1.25 and $1.40. The card for his cousin is $1.50. What is the median price of the birthday cards?

5. What is the median height in your household? How did you decide?

4   DAB • Grade 5 • Unit 1   POPULATIONS AND SAMPLES

Discovery Assignment Book - page 4

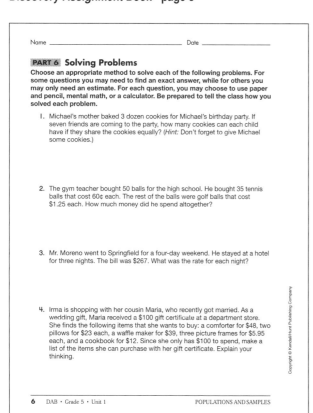

Discovery Assignment Book - page 5

Discovery Assignment Book (p. 5)

Part 4. Addition and Subtraction Practice

A. 114
B. 241
C. 136
D. 7902
E. 8673
F. 11,115
G. 3799
H. 12,601
I. 1926

Part 5. Number of Windows

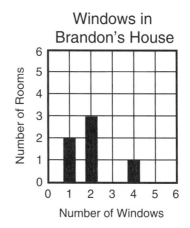

1. 2 windows
2. 12 windows

Discovery Assignment Book (p. 6)

Part 6. Solving Problems

1. 4 cookies each with 4 cookies left or
$4\frac{1}{2}$ cookies each.
2. $39.75
3. $89.00
4. Answers will vary. One possible purchase is
a comforter and two pillows for $94.00.

Discovery Assignment Book - page 6

Glossary

This glossary provides definitions of key vocabulary terms in the Grade 5 lessons. Locations of key vocabulary terms in the curriculum are included with each definition. Components Key: URG = *Unit Resource Guide* and SG = *Student Guide*.

A

Acute Angle (URG Unit 6; SG Unit 6)
An angle that measures less than 90°.

Acute Triangle (URG Unit 6 & Unit 15; SG Unit 6 & Unit 15)
A triangle that has only acute angles.

All-Partials Multiplication Method (URG Unit 2)
A paper-and-pencil method for solving multiplication problems. Each partial product is recorded on a separate line. (*See also* partial product.)

$$\begin{array}{r} 186 \\ \times\ 3 \\ \hline 18 \\ 240 \\ 300 \\ \hline 558 \end{array}$$

Altitude of a Triangle (URG Unit 15; SG Unit 15)
A line segment from a vertex of a triangle perpendicular to the opposite side or to the line extending the opposite side; also, the length of this line. The altitude is also called the height of the triangle.

Angle (URG Unit 6; SG Unit 6)
The amount of turning or the amount of opening between two rays that have the same endpoint.

Arc (URG Unit 14; SG Unit 14)
Part of a circle between two points. (*See also* circle.)

Area (URG Unit 4 & Unit 15; SG Unit 4 & Unit 15)
A measurement of size. The area of a shape is the amount of space it covers, measured in square units.

Average (URG Unit 1 & Unit 4; SG Unit 1 & Unit 4)
A number that can be used to represent a typical value in a set of data. (*See also* mean, median, and mode.)

Axes (URG Unit 10; SG Unit 10)
Reference lines on a graph. In the Cartesian coordinate system, the axes are two perpendicular lines that meet at the origin. The singular of axes is axis.

B

Base of a Triangle (URG Unit 15; SG Unit 15)
One of the sides of a triangle; also, the length of the side. A perpendicular line drawn from the vertex opposite the base is called the height or altitude of the triangle.

Base of an Exponent (URG Unit 2; SG Unit 2)
When exponents are used, the number being multiplied. In $3^4 = 3 \times 3 \times 3 \times 3 = 81$, the 3 is the base and the 4 is the exponent. The 3 is multiplied by itself 4 times.

Base-Ten Pieces (URG Unit 2; SG Unit 2)
A set of manipulatives used to model our number system as shown in the figure below. Note that a skinny is made of 10 bits, a flat is made of 100 bits, and a pack is made of 1000 bits.

Base-Ten Shorthand (URG Unit 2)
A graphical representation of the base-ten pieces as shown below.

Nickname	Picture	Shorthand
bit		
skinny		
flat		
pack		

Benchmarks (SG Unit 7)
Numbers convenient for comparing and ordering numbers, e.g., $0, \frac{1}{2}, 1$ are convenient benchmarks for comparing and ordering fractions.

Best-Fit Line (URG Unit 3; SG Unit 3)
The line that comes closest to the points on a point graph.

Binning Data (URG Unit 8; SG Unit 8)
Placing data from a data set with a large number of values or large range into intervals in order to more easily see patterns in the data.

Bit (URG Unit 2; SG Unit 2)
A cube that measures 1 cm on each edge.
It is the smallest of the base-ten pieces and
is often used to represent 1. (*See also* base-ten pieces.)

C

Cartesian Coordinate System (URG Unit 10;
SG Unit 10)
A method of locating points on a flat surface by means of an ordered pair of numbers. This method is named after its originator, René Descartes. (*See also* coordinates.)

Categorical Variable (URG Unit 1; SG Unit 1)
Variables with values that are not numbers. (*See also* variable and value.)

Center of a Circle (URG Unit 14; SG Unit 14)
The point such that every point on a circle is the same distance from it. (*See also* circle.)

Centiwheel (URG Unit 7; SG Unit 7)
A circle divided into 100 equal sections used in exploring fractions, decimals, and percents.

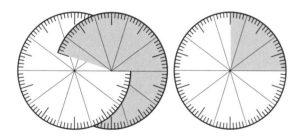

Central Angle (URG Unit 14; SG Unit 14)
An angle whose vertex is at the center of a circle.

Certain Event (URG Unit 7; SG Unit 7)
An event that has a probability of 1 (100%).

Chord (URG Unit 14; SG Unit 14)
A line segment that connects two points on a circle.
(*See also* circle.)

Circle (URG Unit 14; SG Unit 14)
A curve that is made up of all the points that are the same distance from one point, the center.

Circumference (URG Unit 14; SG Unit 14)
The distance around a circle.

Common Denominator (URG Unit 5 & Unit 11;
SG Unit 5 & Unit 11)
A denominator that is shared by two or more fractions. A common denominator is a common multiple of the denominators of the fractions. 15 is a common denominator of $\frac{2}{3} (= \frac{10}{15})$ and $\frac{4}{5} (= \frac{12}{15})$ since 15 is divisible by both 3 and 5.

Common Fraction (URG Unit 7; SG Unit 7)
Any fraction that is written with a numerator and denominator that are whole numbers. For example, $\frac{3}{4}$ and $\frac{9}{4}$ are both common fractions. (*See also* decimal fraction.)

Commutative Property of Addition (URG Unit 2)
The order of the addends in an addition problem does not matter, e.g., $7 + 3 = 3 + 7$.

Commutative Property of Multiplication (URG Unit 2)
The order of the factors in a multiplication problem does not matter, e.g., $7 \times 3 = 3 \times 7$. (*See also* turn-around facts.)

Compact Method (URG Unit 2)
Another name for what is considered the traditional multiplication algorithm.

$$\begin{array}{r} {}^{2}{}^{1}186 \\ \times\ 3 \\ \hline 558 \end{array}$$

Composite Number (URG Unit 11; SG Unit 11)
A number that has more than two distinct factors. For example, 9 has three factors (1, 3, 9) so it is a composite number.

Concentric Circles (URG Unit 14; SG Unit 14)
Circles that have the same center.

Congruent (URG Unit 6 & Unit 10; SG Unit 6)
Figures that are the same shape and size. Polygons are congruent when corresponding sides have the same length and corresponding angles have the same measure.

Conjecture (URG Unit 11; SG Unit 11)
A statement that has not been proved to be true, nor shown to be false.

Convenient Number (URG Unit 2; SG Unit 2)
A number used in computation that is close enough to give a good estimate, but is also easy to compute with mentally, e.g., 25 and 30 are convenient numbers for 27.

Convex (URG Unit 6)
A shape is convex if for any two points in the shape, the line segment between the points is also inside the shape.

Coordinates (URG Unit 10; SG Unit 10)
An ordered pair of numbers that locates points on a flat surface relative to a pair of coordinate axes. For example, in the ordered pair (4, 5), the first number (coordinate) is the distance from the point to the vertical axis and the second coordinate is the distance from the point to the horizontal axis. (*See also* axes.)

Corresponding Parts (URG Unit 10; SG Unit 10)
Matching parts in two or more figures. In the figure below, Sides AB and A′B′ are corresponding parts.

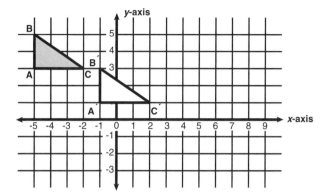

Cryptography (SG Unit 11) The study of secret codes.

Cubic Centimeter (URG Unit 13)
The volume of a cube that is one centimeter long on each edge.

D

Data (SG Unit 1)
Information collected in an experiment or survey.

Decagon (URG Unit 6; SG Unit 6)
A ten-sided, ten-angled polygon.

Decimal (URG Unit 7; SG Unit 7)
1. A number written using the base ten place value system.
2. A number containing a decimal point.

Decimal Fraction (URG Unit 7; SG Unit 7)
A fraction written as a decimal. For example, 0.75 and 0.4 are decimal fractions and $\frac{75}{100}$ and $\frac{4}{10}$ are the equivalent common fractions.

Degree (URG Unit 6; SG Unit 6)
A degree (°) is a unit of measure for angles. There are 360 degrees in a circle.

Denominator (URG Unit 3; SG Unit 3)
The number below the line in a fraction. The denominator indicates the number of equal parts in which the unit whole is divided. For example, the 5 is the denominator in the fraction $\frac{2}{5}$. In this case the unit whole is divided into five equal parts. (*See also* numerator.)

Density (URG Unit 13; SG Unit 13)
The ratio of an object's mass to its volume.

Diagonal (URG Unit 6)
A line segment that connects nonadjacent corners of a polygon.

Diameter (URG Unit 14; SG Unit 14)
1. A line segment that connects two points on a circle and passes through the center.
2. The length of this line segment.

Digit (SG Unit 2)
Any one of the ten symbols 0, 1, 2, 3, 4, 5, 6, 7, 8, 9. The number 37 is made up of the digits 3 and 7.

Dividend (URG Unit 4 & Unit 9; SG Unit 4 & Unit 9)
The number that is divided in a division problem, e.g., 12 is the dividend in 12 ÷ 3 = 4.

Divisor (URG Unit 2, Unit 4, & Unit 9; SG Unit 2, Unit 4, & Unit 9)
In a division problem, the number by which another number is divided. In the problem 12 ÷ 4 = 3, the 4 is the divisor, the 12 is the dividend, and the 3 is the quotient.

Dodecagon (URG Unit 6; SG Unit 6)
A twelve-sided, twelve-angled polygon.

E

Endpoint (URG Unit 6; SG Unit 6)
The point at either end of a line segment or the point at the end of a ray.

Equally Likely (URG Unit 7; SG Unit 7)
When events have the same probability, they are called equally likely.

Equidistant (URG Unit 14)
At the same distance.

Equilateral Triangle (URG Unit 6, Unit 14, & Unit 15)
A triangle that has all three sides equal in length. An equilateral triangle also has three equal angles.

Equivalent Fractions (URG Unit 3; SG Unit 3)
Fractions that have the same value, e.g., $\frac{2}{4} = \frac{1}{2}$.

Estimate (URG Unit 2; SG Unit 2)
1. To find *about* how many (as a verb).
2. A number that is *close to* the desired number (as a noun).

Expanded Form (SG Unit 2)
A way to write numbers that shows the place value of each digit, e.g., 4357 = 4000 + 300 + 50 + 7.

Exponent (URG Unit 2 & Unit 11; SG Unit 2 & Unit 11)
The number of times the base is multiplied by itself. In $3^4 = 3 \times 3 \times 3 \times 3 = 81$, the 3 is the base and the 4 is the exponent. The 3 is multiplied by itself 4 times.

Extrapolation (URG Unit 13; SG Unit 13)
Using patterns in data to make predictions or to estimate values that lie beyond the range of values in the set of data.

F

Fact Families (URG Unit 2; SG Unit 2)
Related math facts, e.g., 3 × 4 = 12, 4 × 3 = 12, 12 ÷ 3 = 4, 12 ÷ 4 = 3.

Factor Tree (URG Unit 11; SG Unit 11)
A diagram that shows the prime factorization of a number.

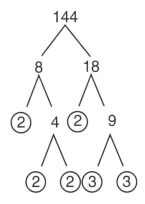

Factors (URG Unit 2 & Unit 11; SG Unit 2 & Unit 11)
1. In a multiplication problem, the numbers that are multiplied together. In the problem $3 \times 4 = 12$, 3 and 4 are the factors.
2. Numbers that divide a number evenly, e.g., 1, 2, 3, 4, 6, and 12 are all the factors of 12.

Fair Game (URG Unit 7; SG Unit 7)
A game in which it is equally likely that any player will win.

Fewest Pieces Rule (URG Unit 2)
Using the least number of base-ten pieces to represent a number. (*See also* base-ten pieces.)

Fixed Variables (URG Unit 4; SG Unit 3 & Unit 4)
Variables in an experiment that are held constant or not changed, in order to find the relationship between the manipulated and responding variables. These variables are often called controlled variables. (*See also* manipulated variable and responding variable.)

Flat (URG Unit 2; SG Unit 2)
A block that measures 1 cm $\times$ 10 cm $\times$ 10 cm. It is one of the base-ten pieces and is often used to represent 100. (*See also* base-ten pieces.)

Flip (URG Unit 10; SG Unit 10)
A motion of the plane in which the plane is reflected over a line so that any point and its image are the same distance from the line.

Forgiving Division Method
(URG Unit 4; SG Unit 4)
A paper-and-pencil method for division in which successive partial quotients are chosen and subtracted from the dividend, until the remainder is less than the divisor. The sum of the partial quotients is the quotient. For example, $644 \div 7$ can be solved as shown at the right.

```
        92
  7 ) 644
      140  | 20
      ---
      504
      350  | 50
      ---
      154
      140  | 20
      ---
       14
       14  |  2
      ---
        0  | 92
```

Formula (SG Unit 11 & Unit 14)
A number sentence that gives a general rule. A formula for finding the area of a rectangle is Area = length $\times$ width, or $A = l \times w$.

Fraction (URG Unit 7; SG Unit 7)
A number that can be written as a/b where a and b are whole numbers and b is not zero.

G

Googol (URG Unit 2)
A number that is written as a 1 with 100 zeroes after it (10^{100}).

Googolplex (URG Unit 2)
A number that is written as a 1 with a googol of zeroes after it.

H

Height of a Triangle (URG Unit 15; SG Unit 15)
A line segment from a vertex of a triangle perpendicular to the opposite side or to the line extending the opposite side; also, the length of this line. The height is also called the altitude.

Hexagon (URG Unit 6; SG Unit 6)
A six-sided polygon.

Hypotenuse (URG Unit 15; SG Unit 15)
The longest side of a right triangle.

I

Image (URG Unit 10; SG Unit 10)
The result of a transformation, in particular a slide (translation) or a flip (reflection), in a coordinate plane. The new figure after the slide or flip is the image of the old figure.

Impossible Event (URG Unit 7; SG Unit 7)
An event that has a probability of 0 or 0%.

Improper Fraction (URG Unit 3; SG Unit 3)
A fraction in which the numerator is greater than or equal to the denominator. An improper fraction is greater than or equal to one.

Infinite (URG Unit 2)
Never ending, immeasurably great, unlimited.

Interpolation (URG Unit 13; SG Unit 13)
Making predictions or estimating values that lie between data points in a set of data.

Intersect (URG Unit 14)
To meet or cross.

Isosceles Triangle (URG Unit 6 & Unit 15)
A triangle that has at least two sides of equal length.

J

K

L

Lattice Multiplication
(URG Unit 9; SG Unit 9)
A method for multiplying that
uses a lattice to arrange the
partial products so the digits are
correctly placed in the correct
place value columns. A lattice
for $43 \times 96 = 4128$ is shown at
the right.

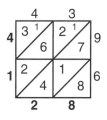

Legs of a Right Triangle (URG Unit 15; SG Unit 15)
The two sides of a right triangle that form the right angle.

Length of a Rectangle (URG Unit 4 & Unit 15;
SG Unit 4 & Unit 15)
The distance along one side of a rectangle.

Line
A set of points that form a straight path extending infinitely in two directions.

Line of Reflection (URG Unit 10)
A line that acts as a mirror so that after a shape is flipped over the line, corresponding points are at the same distance (equidistant) from the line.

Line Segment (URG Unit 14)
A part of a line between and including two points, called the endpoints.

Liter (URG Unit 13)
Metric unit used to measure volume. A liter is a little more than a quart.

Lowest Terms (SG Unit 11)
A fraction is in lowest terms if the numerator and denominator have no common factor greater than 1.

M

Manipulated Variable (URG Unit 4; SG Unit 4)
In an experiment, the variable with values known at the beginning of the experiment. The experimenter often chooses these values before data is collected. The manipulated variable is often called the independent variable.

Mass (URG Unit 13)
The amount of matter in an object.

Mean (URG Unit 1 & Unit 4; SG Unit 1 & Unit 4)
An average of a set of numbers that is found by adding the values of the data and dividing by the number of values.

Measurement Division (URG Unit 4)
Division as equal grouping. The total number of objects and the number of objects in each group are known. The number of groups is the unknown. For example, tulip bulbs come in packages of 8. If 216 bulbs are sold, how many packages are sold?

Median (URG Unit 1; SG Unit 1)
For a set with an odd number of data arranged in order, it is the middle number. For an even number of data arranged in order, it is the mean of the two middle numbers.

Meniscus (URG Unit 13)
The curved surface formed when a liquid creeps up the side of a container (for example, a graduated cylinder).

Milliliter (ml) (URG Unit 13)
A measure of capacity in the metric system that is the volume of a cube that is one centimeter long on each side.

Mixed Number (URG Unit 3; SG Unit 3)
A number that is written as a whole number followed by a fraction. It is equal to the sum of the whole number and the fraction.

Mode (URG Unit 1; SG Unit 1)
The most common value in a data set.

Mr. Origin (URG Unit 10; SG Unit 10)
A plastic figure used to represent the origin of a coordinate system and to indicate the directions of the x- and y- axes. (and possibly the z-axis).

N

N-gon (URG Unit 6; SG Unit 6)
A polygon with N sides.

Negative Number (URG Unit 10; SG Unit 10)
A number less than zero; a number to the left of zero on a horizontal number line.

Nonagon (URG Unit 6; SG Unit 6)
A nine-sided polygon.

Numerator (URG Unit 3; SG Unit 3)
The number written above the line in a fraction. For example, the 2 is the numerator in the fraction $\frac{2}{5}$. In this case, we are interested in two of the five parts. (*See also* denominator.)

Numerical Expression (URG Unit 4; SG Unit 4)
A combination of numbers and operations, e.g.,
$5 + 8 \div 4$.

Numerical Variable (URG Unit 1; SG Unit 1)
Variables with values that are numbers. (*See also* variable and value.)

O

Obtuse Angle (URG Unit 6; SG Unit 6)
An angle that measures more than 90°.

Obtuse Triangle (URG Unit 6 & Unit 15; SG Unit 6 & Unit 15)
A triangle that has an obtuse angle.

Octagon (URG Unit 6; SG Unit 6)
An eight-sided polygon.

Ordered Pair (URG Unit 10; SG Unit 10)
A pair of numbers that gives the coordinates of a point on a grid in relation to the origin. The horizontal coordinate is given first; the vertical coordinate is given second. For example, the ordered pair (5, 3) gives the coordinates of the point that is 5 units to the right of the origin and 3 units up.

Origin (URG Unit 10; SG Unit 10)
The point at which the *x*- and *y*-axes intersect on a coordinate plane. The origin is described by the ordered pair (0, 0) and serves as a reference point so that all the points on the plane can be located by ordered pairs.

P

Pack (URG Unit 2; SG Unit 2)
A cube that measures 10 cm on each edge. It is one of the base-ten pieces and is often used to represent 1000. (*See also* base-ten pieces.)

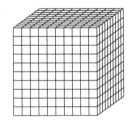

Parallel Lines
(URG Unit 6 & Unit 10)
Lines that are in the same direction. In the plane, parallel lines are lines that do not intersect.

Parallelogram (URG Unit 6)
A quadrilateral with two pairs of parallel sides.

Partial Product (URG Unit 2)
One portion of the multiplication process in the all-partials multiplication method, e.g., in the problem 3×186 there are three partial products: $3 \times 6 = \underline{18}$, $3 \times 80 = \underline{240}$, and $3 \times 100 = \underline{300}$. (*See also* all-partials multiplication method.)

Partitive Division (URG Unit 4)
Division as equal sharing. The total number of objects and the number of groups are known. The number of objects in each group is the unknown. For example, Frank has 144 marbles that he divides equally into 6 groups. How many marbles are in each group?

Pentagon (URG Unit 6; SG Unit 6)
A five-sided polygon.

Percent (URG Unit 7; SG Unit 7)
Per hundred or out of 100. A special ratio that compares a number to 100. For example, 20% (twenty percent) of the jelly beans are yellow means that out of every 100 jelly beans, 20 are yellow.

Perimeter (URG Unit 15; SG Unit 15)
The distance around a two-dimensional shape.

Period (SG Unit 2)
A group of three places in a large number, starting on the right, often separated by commas as shown at the right.

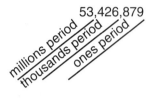

Perpendicular Lines (URG Unit 14 & Unit 15; SG Unit 14)
Lines that meet at right angles.

Pi (π) (URG Unit 14; SG Unit 14)
The ratio of the circumference to diameter of a circle. π = 3.14159265358979. . . . It is a nonterminating, nonrepeating decimal.

Place (SG Unit 2)
The position of a digit in a number.

Place Value (URG Unit 2; SG Unit 2)
The value of a digit in a number. For example, the 5 is in the hundreds place in 4573, so it stands for 500.

Polygon (URG Unit 6; SG Unit 6)
A two-dimensional connected figure made of line segments in which each endpoint of every side meets with an endpoint of exactly one other side.

Population (URG Unit 1 Unit 1)
A collection of persons or things whose properties will be analyzed in a survey or experiment.

Portfolio (URG Unit 2; SG Unit 2)
A collection of student work that show how a student's skills, attitudes, and knowledge change over time.

Positive Number (URG Unit 10; SG Unit 10)
A number greater than zero; a number to the right of zero on a horizontal number line.

Power (URG Unit 2; SG Unit 2)
An exponent. Read 10^4 as, "ten to the fourth power" or "ten to the fourth." We say 10,000 or 10^4 is the fourth power of ten.

Prime Factorization (URG Unit 11; SG Unit 11)
Writing a number as a product of primes. The prime factorization of 100 is $2 \times 2 \times 5 \times 5$.

Prime Number (URG Unit 11; SG Unit 11)
A number that has exactly two factors: itself and 1. For example, 7 has exactly two distinct factors, 1 and 7.

Probability (URG Unit 7; SG Unit 1 & Unit 7)
A number from 0 to 1 (0% to 100%) that describes how likely an event is to happen. The closer that the probability of an event is to one, the more likely the event will happen.

Product (URG Unit 2; SG Unit 2)
The answer to a multiplication problem. In the problem $3 \times 4 = 12$, 12 is the product.

Proper Fraction (URG Unit 3; SG Unit 3)
A fraction in which the numerator is less than the denominator. Proper fractions are less than one.

Proportion (URG Unit 3 & Unit 13; SG Unit 13)
A statement that two ratios are equal.

Protractor (URG Unit 6; SG Unit 6)
A tool for measuring angles.

Q

Quadrants (URG Unit 10; SG Unit 10)
The four sections of a coordinate grid that are separated by the axes.

Quadrilateral (URG Unit 6; SG Unit 6)
A polygon with four sides. (*See also* polygon.)

Quotient (URG Unit 4 & Unit 9; SG Unit 2, Unit 4, & Unit 9)
The answer to a division problem. In the problem $12 \div 3 = 4$, the 4 is the quotient.

R

Radius (URG Unit 14; SG Unit 14)
1. A line segment connecting the center of a circle to any point on the circle.
2. The length of this line segment.

Ratio (URG Unit 3 & Unit 12; SG Unit 3 & Unit 13)
A way to compare two numbers or quantities using division. It is often written as a fraction.

Ray (URG Unit 6; SG Unit 6)
A part of a line with one endpoint that extends indefinitely in one direction.

Rectangle (URG Unit 6; SG Unit 6)
A quadrilateral with four right angles.

Reflection (URG Unit 10)
(*See* flip.)

Regular Polygon (URG Unit 6; SG Unit 6; DAB Unit 6)
A polygon with all sides of equal length and all angles equal.

Remainder (URG Unit 4 & Unit 9; SG Unit 4 & Unit 9)
Something that remains or is left after a division problem. The portion of the dividend that is not evenly divisible by the divisor, e.g., $16 \div 5 = 3$ with 1 as a remainder.

Repeating Decimals (SG Unit 9)
A decimal fraction with one or more digits repeating without end.

Responding Variable (URG Unit 4; SG Unit 4)
The variable whose values result from the experiment. Experimenters find the values of the responding variable by doing the experiment. The responding variable is often called the dependent variable.

Rhombus (URG Unit 6; SG Unit 6)
A quadrilateral with four equal sides.

Right Angle (URG Unit 6; SG Unit 6)
An angle that measures 90°.

Right Triangle (URG Unit 6 & Unit 15; SG Unit 6 & Unit 15)
A triangle that contains a right angle.

Rubric (URG Unit 1)
A scoring guide that can be used to guide or assess student work.

S

Sample (URG Unit 1)
A part or subset of a population.

Scalene Triangle (URG Unit 15)
A triangle that has no sides that are equal in length.

Scientific Notation (URG Unit 2; SG Unit 2)
A way of writing numbers, particularly very large or very small numbers. A number in scientific notation has two factors. The first factor is a number greater than or equal to one and less than ten. The second factor is a power of 10 written with an exponent. For example, 93,000,000 written in scientific notation is 9.3×10^7.

Septagon (URG Unit 6; SG Unit 6)
A seven-sided polygon.

Side-Angle-Side (URG Unit 6 & Unit 14)
A geometric property stating that two triangles having two corresponding sides with the included angle equal are congruent.

Side-Side-Side (URG Unit 6)
A geometric property stating that two triangles having corresponding sides equal are congruent.

Sides of an Angle (URG Unit 6; SG Unit 6)
The sides of an angle are two rays with the same endpoint. (*See also* endpoint and ray.)

Sieve of Eratosthenes (SG Unit 11)
A method for separating prime numbers from nonprime numbers developed by Eratosthenes, an Egyptian librarian, in about 240 BCE.

Similar (URG Unit 6; SG Unit 6)
Similar shapes have the same shape but not necessarily the same size.

Skinny (URG Unit 2; SG Unit 2)
A block that measures 1 cm × 1 cm × 10 cm.
It is one of the base-ten pieces
and is often used to represent 10.
(*See also* base-ten pieces.)

Slide (URG Unit 10; SG Unit 10)
Moving a geometric figure in the plane by moving every
point of the figure the same distance in the same direction. Also called translation.

Speed (URG Unit 3 & Unit 5; SG Unit 3 & Unit 5)
The ratio of distance moved to time taken, e.g.,
3 miles/1 hour or 3 mph is a speed.

Square (URG Unit 6 & Unit 14; SG Unit 6)
A quadrilateral with four equal sides and four right
angles.

Square Centimeter (URG Unit 4; SG Unit 4)
The area of a square that is 1 cm long on each side.

Square Number (URG Unit 11)
A number that is the product of a whole number multiplied by itself. For example, 25 is a square number since
$5 \times 5 = 25$. A square number can be represented by a
square array with the same number of rows as columns.
A square array for 25 has 5 rows of 5 objects in each row
or 25 total objects.

Standard Form (SG Unit 2)
The traditional way to write a number, e.g., standard
form for three hundred fifty-seven is 357. (*See also*
expanded form and word form.)

Standard Units (URG Unit 4)
Internationally or nationally agreed-upon units used in
measuring variables, e.g., centimeters and inches are
standard units used to measure length and square centimeters and square inches are used to measure area.

Straight Angle (URG Unit 6; SG Unit 6)
An angle that measures 180º.

T

Ten Percent (URG Unit 4; SG Unit 4)
10 out of every hundred or $\frac{1}{10}$.

Tessellation (URG Unit 6 & Unit 10; SG Unit 6)
A pattern made up of one or more repeated shapes that
completely covers a surface without any gaps or overlaps.

Translation
(*See* slide.)

Trapezoid (URG Unit 6)
A quadrilateral with exactly one pair of parallel sides.

Triangle (URG Unit 6; SG Unit 6)
A polygon with three sides.

Triangulating (URG Unit 6; SG Unit 6)
Partitioning a polygon into two or more nonoverlapping
triangles by drawing diagonals that do not intersect.

Turn-Around Facts (URG Unit 2)
Multiplication facts that have the same factors but in a
different order, e.g., $3 \times 4 = 12$ and $4 \times 3 = 12$.
(*See also* commutative property of multiplication.)

Twin Primes (URG Unit 11; SG Unit 11)
A pair of prime numbers whose difference is 2.
For example, 3 and 5 are twin primes.

U

Unit Ratio (URG Unit 13; SG Unit 13)
A ratio with a denominator of one.

V

Value (URG Unit 1; SG Unit 1)
The possible outcomes of a variable. For example, red,
green, and blue are possible values for the variable *color*.
Two meters and 1.65 meters are possible values for the
variable *length*.

Variable (URG Unit 1; SG Unit 1)
1. An attribute or quantity that changes or varies.
   (*See also* categorical variable and numerical variable.)
2. A symbol that can stand for a variable.

Variables in Proportion (URG Unit 13; SG Unit 13)
When the ratio of two variables in an experiment is
always the same, the variables are in proportion.

Velocity (URG Unit 5; SG Unit 5)
Speed in a given direction. Speed is the ratio of the distance traveled to time taken.

Vertex (URG Unit 6; SG Unit 6)
A common point of two rays or line segments that form
an angle.

Volume (URG Unit 13)
The measure of the amount of space occupied by an
object.

W

Whole Number
Any of the numbers 0, 1, 2, 3, 4, 5, 6 and so on.

Width of a Rectangle (URG Unit 4 & Unit 15;
    SG Unit 4 & Unit 15)
The distance along one side of a rectangle is the length
and the distance along an adjacent side is the width.

Word Form (SG Unit 2)
A number expressed in words, e.g., the word form for
123 is "one hundred twenty-three." (*See also* expanded
form and standard form.)

X

Y

Z